An Honest Look at Life:
Studies in Ecclesiastes

Harold T. Bryson

An Honest Look at Life:
Studies in Ecclesiastes

Harold T. Bryson

Mossy Creek Press

Copyright (C) 2011 by Harold T. Bryson

ISBN: Softcover   978-1-936912-30-8

All rights reserved. No part of this book may be reproduced or transmitted in any form or by any means, electronic or mechanical, including photocopying, recording, or by any information storage and retrieval system, without permission in writing from the publisher.

This book was printed in the United States of America.

All Scripture is NRSV.

Profits from the sale of this book goes to support students at Carson-Newman College through scholarships and student ministries.

To order additional copies of this book, contact:

Mossy Creek Press
1-423-475-7308
www.mossycreekpress.com

Dedicated
to
Richard (Mugsy) Davis

Contents

Chapter 1
A Background of Ecclesiastes 1:1   9

Chapter 2
A Personal Ventilation about Life   36
1:2–11

Chapter 3
An Autobiography of an Illustrious Life   53
1:12–2:26

Chapter 4
An Observation of an Ordered Universe   76
3:1–15

Chapter 5
A Look at Human Relationships   91
3:16–4:16

Chapter 6
The Sight of Attendants at the House of God   106
5:1–7

Chapter 7

A Glimpse of People's Mania for Money   119
5:8–20

Chapter 8

The Sight of Disappointed People   131
6:1–12

Chapter 9

An Insight into What Is Good for People   143
7:1–8:1

Chapter 10

A Reflection about Coping with Life   163
8:2–17

Chapter 11

A Final, Honest Appraisal of Life   177
9:1–18

Chapter 12

A Scrutiny of Foolish People   192
10:1–20

Chapter 13

A Glimpse at a Better Life   204
11:1–10

Chapter 14

An Insight into the Creator of Life 219
12:1–14

Works Cited 235

End Notes 239

Chapter 1
A Background of Ecclesiastes
1:1

The book of Ecclesiastes has been deemed one of the strangest books in the Bible. Its author invites readers to look at various sights of life he had seen and to think with him about them. We do not even know this author's name. The Jews called him Qohelet. The Greeks translated Qohelet as Koheleth or Ecclesiastes. These names speak of a task a person performed. He is one who calls an audience together and talks with them about various topics. Usually the Teacher was one who had accumulated much wisdom and wealth and was a greatly respected person. This author of Ecclesiastes, whose pen name is Koheleth or Teacher, has been considered to be unusual because he was outspoken, controversial, incisive, and nontraditional. But for centuries individuals and groups have read the writing of this Teacher and listened, questioned, agreed, and pondered.

Readers of Ecclesiastes immediately recognize the strange and disquieting content of the book. The writer verbalizes observations and experiences not usually thought of as religious: the pain and frustration engendered by an unblinking glaze at life's absurdities and injustices. He observes issues of life distressing to see: the apparent meaninglessness of life, the dissatisfaction with human accomplishments, the emptiness of pleasure, death as the final end with the encouragement to eat, drink, and be merry since the present is all we have, and the unfair injustices scattered throughout the landscape of life. Koheleth looks at life honestly, truthfully, experientially, globally and reports his facts and ventilates his feelings. He speaks about life "under the sun," an expression used twenty-nine times in Ecclesiastes. The expression is unique to Koheleth. It refers to a perspective of life based on earthly experiences and observations.

Koheleth has some unusual insights about life, and his views should not be forced to say what people want him to say. Koheleth's theology represents one person's view of the world and his glimpse of God. His truths are partial, and his thinking is a process. He observes life's injustices and absurdities and refuses to impose pat answers on them. In all of his observations and experiences of life, he maintains a faith in the sovereignty of God, and he looks for ways to have a meaningful life in a world where so much is senseless.[1]

Readers of Ecclesiastes not only confront unusual themes and content, but they also encounter a unique writing style. Koheleth does not think or reason methodically. He has not worked out a systematic worldview or theology and presented them in an organized form. Instead, he expresses his thoughts with irregularity and repetition. He struggles with his observations of life and his beliefs. Some of his ideas go in opposite directions and run counter to familiar wisdom literature. The serious student of Ecclesiastes will need to cope with Koheleth's contradictions, trace his arguments, decipher his imagery, and accept his exaggerations. The book lies before the reader like a chest full of puzzles, testing us each time we try to work the puzzle. Partial understanding is all we can hope, but that is the case in most of what we do.[2]

Though Ecclesiastes may be difficult and different both in content and style, it belongs in the canon of Scripture and deserves serious study. Koheleth looked at life in the times in which he lived. He faced life's inequities and absurdities. He refused to teach easy answers for the living of life. But he did maintain faith in God's rule and fundamental justice.

Looking at Koheleth's observations of life then seems to differ little from looking at life now. Injustices exist today in terrorism, white-collar cheating, sexual abuse, exploitation of the poor, armed robberies, senseless murders, and the list continues. Many live life today in a secularistic mind-set thinking primarily of money, sex, and power. Any observant person realizes we live in a world affected by postmodernity. Many ancient axioms and virtuous values have been challenged or abandoned. Reading and studying Ecclesiastes will help us to look at life "under the sun," or life from the perspective of a purely earthly existence. But Ecclesiastes will afford opportunities to think about a better life coming from "beyond the sun."

Any study of a Bible book must begin with the book's original background. It originated in a time long ago and in a place far away. It came into being because of a life situation that needed to be addressed with a word from the Lord. God inspired Koheleth to look at life honestly and to keep his faith. Our background study begins with issues about the original human author.

Author

Ecclesiastes begins with a title verse or what is commonly called a superscription. "The words of the Teacher, the son of David, king in Jerusalem" (1:1). The English title of Ecclesiastes has been handed down from the Septuagint (*ekkesiastes*) to the Latin Vulgate (*Liber Ecclesiastes*). The Greek title gives the name of the main speaker of the book who calls himself ekkesiastes. This Greek name is a translation of the Hebrew qohelet. Qohelet is not a proper name but rather a nickname of sorts that functions as a type of pseudonym. The name literally means "one who assembles."

Oftentimes the name/title is called "the Preacher" or "the Teacher." Most Old Testament scholars think that Qohelet was too nontraditional to be calling a religious assembly together. They believe the group he assembled was a classroom of sorts, thus they translate Qohelet as "Teacher." More than likely Oohelet does mean "one who teaches the public." For the sake of consistency, the Greek rendering Koheleth will be used in this study instead of the Hebrew word Qohelet. The word Teacher will be the choice rather than Preacher.

The title verse indicates two truths about the author. First, he is a Teacher who shares truth with the public. Second, he calls himself "the son of David, king in Jerusalem." Koheleth has traditionally been identified with Solomon on the basis in this title verse in 1:1 and another reference in 1:12. "I, the Teacher, when king over Israel in Jerusalem." This identification of "son of David, king in Jerusalem," along with other factors, has caused scholars through the years to identify Solomon as the author of Ecclesiastes. Others factors associate the book with Solomon. The author includes many proverbs in Ecclesiastes. In biblical tradition, Solomon is described as the consummate patron of wisdom (1 Kings 3-4), having composed three thousand proverbs and 1,005 songs. He describes himself as having great experience with wisdom

An Honest Look at Life: Ecclesiastes

and knowledge (cf. 1:16). Also, the writer of Ecclesiastes tells of building houses, planting vineyards, making gardens, and irrigating an entire forest (2:4-6). He relates the greatness of his wealth (2:7, 9) and the abundance of his concubines (2:8). These characteristics do fit the life of Solomon. Therefore, on the basis of this information Solomon has traditionally been considered the author of Ecclesiastes. One opinion holds that Solomon wrote Ecclesiastes in his old age, and indeed Koheleth gives the impression of speaking from the vantage point of an older person looking back at life.[3]

As centuries passed, for various reasons Bible students began to reevaluate the traditional view of the author of Ecclesiastes. Martin Luther in the sixteenth century asserted a non-Solomon authorship for the book. Various problems presented by other scholars gave legitimate reasons to question Solomon as the author of Ecclesiastes. First, the book's Hebrew language and background indicate a date later than Solomon. Scholars discovered more about ancient customs of writing and developments in the Hebrew language. The syntax and vocabulary in Ecclesiastes have noticeable differences than in early Hebrew. Second, Solomon could not have made several statements in the book. Solomon was king until his death, but in the title verse of 1:1, the writer implies that he was no longer king. Third, the name of Solomon does not appear in Ecclesiastes while his name appears in both

Proverbs and Song of Solomon. Fourth, Koheleth blames the royal government for social injustices (5:7). This was something Solomon, who was involved in the government, would not have done.

After Luther questioned Solomon as the single author of Ecclesiastes, various speculations began to arise about the identity of the author. Temper Longman III thinks the nickname Koheleth was adopted by the actual writer to associate himself with Solomon while retaining his distance from the actual person. He says, "It is a way of indicating that the Solomonic persona is being adopted for literary and communicative purposes."[4] Longman thinks Koheleth pretends to be Solomon while he explores avenues of meaning in the world. Solomon had the reputation of being the richest and wisest man in the world, and if he could not find meaning in the things of the world, who could?[5]

The implicit references to Solomon in Ecclesiastes need to be noticed. The association of the Teacher or Koheleth with Solomon serves as an important function in the book. The Teacher assumes the character of Solomon in order to explore areas of potential meaning. Of course the author had no intent to deceive the readers. From the historical record of the Kings material we know that Solomon had more of everything than anyone else did, but the end of his life ended in meaninglessness.

Other scholars suggest that two, three, or as many as nine different minds had a part in writing the book.[6] Most Old Testament scholars seem to have a consensus for a single author of Ecclesiastes with one or two editors writing the epilogue of 12:8–14 and perhaps the prologue of 1:1–11. Both the prologue and the epilogue are written in the third person instead of the first person that prevails in the body of Ecclesiastes.

Well, who wrote the book of Ecclesiastes? Solomon? Two, three, or more authors? As long as Bible study exists "under the sun," many will assert that Solomon wrote Ecclesiastes. And others will conclude that the book may reference Solomon, but it was written by another person at a time later than Solomon. Does it matter? Of course it does not. What the author wrote matters much more than the one who wrote it. In the final analysis, the book of Ecclesiastes, like many other Old Testament books, is anonymous. But, because of its presence in the canon of Holy Scripture, we can affirm the ultimate prime mover of Ecclesiastes is God. Long ago God spoke through a human author or authors to address a life situation. This writer thinks the author was not Solomon. A writer used Solomon's experience as the backdrop for his argument. Some wise man illustrated the limits of wisdom, pleasure, prestige, wealth, and achievements by citing Solomon's experiences. He "donned Solomon's robes to explore the deficiencies of a way of life based on Solomonic values."[7]

If one day archaeologists discover empirical evidence that either Solomon was or was not the author, this writer will continue to value the words of Koheleth as "the word of God."

Readers and Date

The book of Ecclesiastes contains no explicit indication of the original date of the document or the first readers. Internal evidences within the book give some indications of the general period in which it was written and the possible original readers.

Learning the readers and date of Ecclesiastes link closely with the examination about the author. If Solomon was the author, the original readers would have been Israel during the period of Hebrew history known as the United Kingdom. Solomon lived in the tenth century BC, and if he wrote the book, it would have been dated near the end of his life. The book would be addressed to the Israelites who lived in a great economic, political, and religious time in their history. The time of Solomon in the tenth century does not match many of the ideas in Ecclesiastes. An optimistic attitude prevailed during Solomon's time. Solomon's time coupled with David has been called "the golden age" of Israel's history. It was a time of great literary activity. Excitement prevailed when the temple was completed and dedicated. Wealth and splendor existed throughout the land. The words of Koleleth in

Ecclesiastes indicate a more pessimistic mood. The book of Ecclesiastes simply does not seem to fit the age of Solomon.

A later date than Solomon fits the environment reflected in Ecclesiastes much better. A postexilic date seems to fit the conditions reflected in the book. Roger Whybray writes, "The book was written many centuries after Solomon, most probably in the third century B.C. The main reasons for this dating are three: the character of the Hebrew in which it is written, its mood and style of argument, and its place in the history of thought. Each of these considerations would be sufficient in itself to prove that it is one of the latest compositions in the Old Testament."[8] Whybray suggests that the book was probably written "when Palestine was ruled from Egypt by the Ptolemaic dynasty.[9]

Beginning in the Persian period (539–337 BC), certain sociological and economic developments occurred that dramatically and indelibly changed the environment of Palestine. In contrast to the largely agrarian activity of preexilic Judah, the economy became more commercialized in the fifth century. A standard monetary currency was introduced for the first time in order to help trade from Egypt to Persia. A new economy emerged with many entrepreneurial opportunities. But this economic growth did not benefit all the people. The rich had unprecedented opportunities for becoming richer. Those of lesser financial means had a distinct disadvantage. The middle class became overwhelmed with the abundance of economic opportunities and risks. A person could reap profit one day and lose a lot the next day.[10]

Another main reason for adopting a late date is the language of Ecclesiastes. The closeness of Koheleth's language with that of the Mishnah, which was compiled in approximately 200 AD, marks differences in the Hebrew in Ecclesiastes and classical Hebrew. It indicates that the book was not written at the beginning of the period of classical Hebrew (the time of Solomon) but many centuries later when the long-lived classical pattern of the language had already undergone considerable change.

The presence of two Persian words in the text of Ecclesiastes could also indicate a date after the rise of the Persian Empire in the sixth century BC. Some scholars have suggested Greek linguistic influences, but this is hard to prove with certainty. The vocabulary, grammar, and syntax resemble late Hebrew and Aramaic, and this argument pushed scholars to prefer a late date for the book.

Another evidence for a late date of Ecclesiastes is the mood reflected in the book. The time reflected in Ecclesiastes is one of misery and vanity (1:2–11); the splendor of Solomon's era was gone (1:12–2:26); a time of

An Honest Look at Life: Ecclesiastes

death had begun for Israel (3:1-15); injustice and violence were present (4:1-3); there was heathen tyranny (5:7, 9-19); death was preferred to life (7:1); and one man ruled over other men to their hurt (8:9). These pessimistic tones represent a time different from the optimistic age of Solomon. The original readers, according to evidences within Ecclesiastes, seem to live amid the mood of cynicism, pessimism, and skepticism.

Historical happenings in Judah of nearly three centuries helped to shape the pessimism present in the readers. Three hundred years of being ruled by various foreign powers created faded memories of independence and the absence of a national destiny. This historical setting had all but robbed the people and their leaders of the vibrant life with God that pulsates in the Psalms and the Prophets. In Judah's exilic period skepticism developed toward the competence of wisdom and the unfailing success of righteousness. Koheleth's time seems to indicate the absence and inactivity of God. Arrogant religious leaders sought to explain life's crises with simple formulas. These formulas offered promises that could not be delivered. Earlier in Judah's history teachers of wisdom advocated prosperity as proof of righteousness. Good conduct, according to these thinkers, resulted in a long life. Koheleth sees that both injustice and death sever the ties between responsible behavior and desirable outcome. The old formulas had failed to explain life. Koheleth looked honestly at life and sought a better way to deal with life's realities and absurdities.

Ecclesiastes seems to be a work of the later postexilic period. The old values of Israelite society had been largely set aside as a result of the influences of other cultures. A new spirit of materialistic enterprise motive by the Ptolemies emerged. Its language marks the book as one of the latest books written in the Old Testament. These evidence indicate a date in the late Persian period or the early stages of the Seleucid Greek regime. This would date Ecclesiastes in the third or fourth century BC.

Various places have been proposed as the place of the composition of Ecclesiastes. Although some have argued for a place of writing outside Palestine, more evidence in the book seems to point to Palestine. The references to weather conditions such as the unpredictability of the weather, dependence on rainfall, the direction of the wind (11:4), and successions of rainstorms do not correspond to climate conditions in Egypt. Furthermore, the almond tree, which was mentioned several times in the Old Testament as growing in Palestine, was not found in Egypt. Among local customs mentioned by Koheleth, we find several characteristics of Palestine but improbable in Egypt. Equally decisive for a Palestinian origin are the references to the temple.[11]

Purpose

No book in the Bible just happened. In every book in the Bible, God inspired human authors to address a heavenly message for an earthly need. Why did Koheleth write Ecclesiastes? He does not state an explicit purpose at any place in the book. But reading Ecclesiastes causes one to see implicit statements that indicate reasons for writing the book. Without a doubt God inspired Koheleth to address human needs either in Solomon's time or in a postexilic time. Reading Ecclesiastes causes one to conclude that these original readers lived in a secular society, that is, culture primarily interested in the accumulation of riches and the pursuit of pleasure. God seemed to be distant and irrelevant to this culture. They had lost their theological moorings on life. They thought life was just to be lived on a horizontal existence, that is, "under the sun."

The Teacher's purpose, then, was to show the readers the deficiency of this secular worldview. Koheleth exhorts Israelites struggling with the meaning of life and God's purposes to pursue wisdom by allowing their thinking to be shaped by the recognition of God as Creator. Then they can enjoy God's good gifts and obey his laws amid the enigma of his purposes.[12]

Perhaps the basic purpose of the book is to get people to think about life lived on earth. Readers of Ecclesiastes found themselves questioning why the faith and certainties so beautifully stated in many parts of the Old Testament seem missing from Ecclesiastes. For example, the psalmist sees creation around him and reflects on what God has done for his people. But Koheleth examines the same world and finds it an unending round of meaninglessness. Also the prophets called for reform of an unjust society, but the Teacher looks at the same kind of unjust society, shrugs his shoulders, and says, "It's the system. You can't beat it" (cf. Ecclesiastes 5:8).[13]

Looking at life honestly and thinking about it seriously is the heart of Koheleth. He looks at life and becomes puzzled. He hears that the righteous should be rewarded and the wicked punished. He thinks the one who toils should enjoy the fruit of his or labors. He thinks the wise should have a life the polar opposite of the fool's life. He believes something should distinguish the righteous from the wicked after death. As Koheleth looked at life, he did not see a strict correspondence between deed and consequence, virtue and reward, vice and punishment. But the Teacher does not see that kind of world. Contradictions appear in the everyday world, and life's meaning seems to collapse. In Ecclesiastes the reader hears a frustrated person struggling with life issues. A basic purpose of his book is to get readers to struggle mentally with him.[14]

The struggle for meaning lies in the heart of the Teacher and appears throughout the book. Koheleth offers subtle pointers as the only hope for meaning and purpose in a messed-up world. He looks at life and describes the senselessness of a despairing world apart from God. Koheleth points beyond pessimism, meaninglessness, senselessness, and despair to give readers occasional glimpses of God. The book ends with three expressions that point away from skeptical thinking and toward a theology resonant with the rest of the Old Testament—"Fear God," "Keep his commandments," and "God will bring every act to judgment" (Eccl. 12:13-14).

So ultimately the purpose of Ecclesiastes is to point beyond a life lived on the horizontal level of "under the sun" to a life on the vertical dimension, namely with God. The Teacher exposes the deficiency of a secular worldview. It results in pessimism, cynicism, skepticism, and many other negative notions. Koheleth gives a gentle nudge for readers to look beyond "life under the sun" and to see life with God "under the sun." Koheleth exhorts Israelites and others struggling with the nature of life's meaning to pursue God's wisdom and allow their thinking to be shaped by the recognition of God as Creator, Sovereign Lord, Gracious Giver, and Infinite Wisdom. Recognizing God during life's experiences will allow people to enjoy God's good gifts and obey his laws amidst the absurdities of life.[15]

Structure

Biblical writers generally used a plan to communicate their content. Unfortunately, determining the overall structure of Ecclesiastes has proven to be notoriously difficult. Efforts to provide an analysis of the contents of Ecclesiastes range from claims that the book is a systematic treatise logically developed with a discernable plan to proposals that Koheleth thoughts ramble, repeat, contradict, and have no organic connection or all-embracing plan. Phyllis Trible says the book "resists organization."[16]

A simple structure seems to appear in three parts: a prologue (1:1–11), a body of life observations (1:12–12:7), and an epilogue (12:8–14). The prologue and the epilogue differ from the main body of the book in that the body of the book uses the first-person reference to Koheleth while the prologue and the epilogue use the third-person singular pronoun. Between the "bookends" of prologue and epilogue, Koheleth looks at life and searches for its meaning. In the main body readers see the Teacher's observations and his feelings about various areas of life.

Ecclesiastes opens with a prologue where a dominant theme for the book appears. "All is vanity." The word "vanity" appears thirty-eight times in the book disclosing Koheleth's pessimism as he looked at life. Throughout the main body of the book, the Teacher gives gentle

An Honest Look at Life: Ecclesiastes

encouragements to fear God (3:14; 5:7; 7:18; 8:12-13). In the epilogue the narrator summarizes Koheleth's reflections and comes to a conclusion about life's meaning. Through many observations and looks for meaning in life, the pattern in Ecclesiastes progresses to the final exhortation: "Fear God and keep his commandments" (12:13).

The structure of Ecclesiastes used in this commentary is the descriptions of a philosopher/theologian's view about the downside and upsides of life. The Teacher may be characterized as a confused wise man. He is someone who knows the wisdom teachings of Israel, but he sets out to understand life on his own. He becomes frustrated and confused by life's incongruities and mysteries. He contradicts himself often as he turned on some occasions to traditional wisdom for answers and at other times to his own observations and reflections of life. After studying the superscription of 1:1, thirteen topics will be studied to learn Koheleth's sights, soundings, and feelings about life. The flow of Ecclesiastes represents a "think along." Koheleth reports much of his inner life and his observations, and he turns to his readers to think with him about what he has seen about life.

Genre

The book of Ecclesiastes comes as close to a philosophical approach to life and truth as any other book in the Bible. Koheleth does not come with many conclusions based on revelation but on observations and experiences. Ecclesiastes belongs to a type of literature known as Wisdom Literature. Certain Psalms, the Song of Solomon, Job, Proverbs, and Ecclesiastes share a wisdom style and content. Wisdom literature focuses on such topics as instructions for successful living and perplexing topics involving the significance and meaning of life.

William LaSor writes about how Near Eastern wisdom literature appears in two types. First, proverbial wisdom made up of "short, pithy sayings which state rules for personal happiness and welfare or condenses the wisdom of experience and makes acute observations about life." Second, "contemplative or speculative wisdom-- written in monologue, dialogue, or essays which delve into basic problems of human existence such as the meaning of life and the problem of suffering." Proverbs represents an example of the first type of wisdom and Job the second. Ecclesiastes contains both types with speculative wisdom in the first half of the book and proverbial wisdom emerging into larger play in the second half.[17]

While the broad genre of Ecclesiastes is wisdom literature, sub-genres exist, and attention needs to be paid to these literary forms. Temper Longman III identifies four of the most common sub-genres as reflection, proverb, anecdote, and wisdom instruction.[18] Sidney Greidanus notices three other literary types: autobiographical narration, metaphor, and allegory.[19] In reflection the author states an observation or truth which he then in turn ponders and evaluates (cf. 1:5; 1:13-15; 1:16-18; 2:1-11; 2:12-17). A proverb is a pithy, highly stylized statement about some area of living (cf. 1:15; 1:18; 4:5; 7:1-12). The most prominent type of proverb in the book is the "better than" proverbs which compare and contrast two states of affairs. An anecdote is a short story told in order to illustrate a truth (cf. 2:21; 4:7-8; 4:13-16; 9:13-16; 10:5-7). An instruction is a teaching in which the author tries to turn his readers toward or away from a line of thinking or course of behavior (cf. 5:1-2).

Koheleth also gives his observations about life by autobiographical narration. In three places a person, historical or fiction, relates his experiences and draws lessons from them. The Teacher's identification as a king speaks about his search for satisfaction and reports the conclusions of his search. Two autobiographical narratives appear in 1:12-2:16 and 7:23-29. Metaphors appear several places in Ecclesiastes. One kind of object or idea is used in place of another to suggest likeness or analogy between them. For example, the writer used four metaphors to describe death: the snapping of a silver cord, the breaking of a golden bowl, the breaking of a pitcher at a fountain, and the breaking of a wheel at a cistern (cf. 12;6). The most repeated metaphor is the Hebrew word *hebel* (translated "vanity"), which compares life to a vapor or breath. One allegory, which is an extended metaphor, appears in 12:3-4 where an elderly person is described in terms of a house and its occupants.

Relevance

Koheleth's world did not differ drastically from today's world. This means it is not a difficult task to apply the words in Ecclesiastes to the twenty-first century. Numerous thought patterns affect thinking in today's world such as secularism, naturalism, postmodernism, agnosticism, pluralism, existentialism, and many others. Human actions arise from the influence of consumerism, hedonism, humanism, terrorism, sadism, and other thought patterns. Many moods appear in today's world such as cynicism, pessimism, criticism, negativism, and skepticism. In such a time people need to hear a word from God. It addresses the crucial questions of our day: Why am I here? What is the meaning of life? Are work, education, pleasure, fame, and wealth all there is to life? Why is life so unfair? Koheleth takes an honest look at life. Students of Koheleth will find themselves thinking along with him. If Ecclesiastes does anything, it causes the reader to look honestly at life and to think seriously about it. The ways Koheleth makes us think underscores the contemporary relevance of the book.

Ecclesiastes causes us to think about the meaninglessness and the meaningfulness of life. The Teacher begins his writing by saying, "Vanity of vanities! All is vanity!" (1:2b). In the conclusion of his book, he writes, "Vanity of vanity, says the Teacher, all is vanity" (12:8). The word translated "vanity"(*hebel*) can mean meaninglessness or absurdity. Michael Fox thinks that *hebel* is best rendered as "absurdity."[20]

The Hebrew language does not have a superlative form as English does. When, for example, we say that "she is the fastest athlete on the field," it indicates that she is the best. The title *Song of Songs* means that it is the best of all songs. And it is clear from the Teacher's repeated use of hebel that he is talking about something that is most absurd or meaningless. And that is *hebel* or meaningless? Life's activities and ultimate death. Koheleth looks at life closely with a lot of its activities and finds it to be absurd, meaningless.

Contemporary literature, plays, and movies reflect the nature of a Western culture in which meaninglessness saps the energy and robs the joy of life. The plight of T. S. Eliot's, "Hollow Man," Arthur Miller's character Willie Loman in the play Death of a Salesman, and the blurring of truth in George Orwell's *1984* testify to a time of apparent absurdity or meaninglessness.

Fortunately, Koheleth did not become a nihilist, which is a belief that all earthly existence is meaningless. The Teacher does find some life meaningful: moderate work, temperate enjoyment of pleasure, love and friendship, gaining and using wisdom. Someone heard Koheleth's evaluation and sensed his struggle and offered a conclusion about meaningfulness in life. Fearing God, obeying his commandments, and living in awareness of God's ultimate judgment encompasses the ultimate meaning of life.

Koheleth causes us to think about the inability of human wisdom and the ability of divine wisdom. Koheleth repeatedly refers to human wisdom as being "under the sun." The author employs "under the sun" to indicate something on earth from an earthly perspective. Human wisdom is limited. It does not have the ability to understand or to interpret life. It is inadequate to explain the meaning of existence. From Koheleth's "under the sun" perspective he lacked the key to unlock the answer to life.

Underlying the Teacher's observation is the idea that from a purely earthly viewpoint all is meaningless, vain, absurd. But also underlying Koheleth's observation is the divine perspective that appears occasionally throughout Ecclesiastes. God's wisdom becomes most pronounced in the epilogue (12:13-14). Basic to Koheleth's thought is that God is in heaven and we are on earth. We see life from earth's perspective. God sees life from his perspective. We evaluate the meaning of life from the perspective of what we see, hear, and experience. But God sees the perfect picture from what be considered as an "above the sun" perspective.

Reading Ecclesiastes prompts us to think about life now and death later. Koheleth thinks a lot about death. For him death is an ultimate absurdity, especially from his "under the sun" perspective. From his viewpoint life is brief no hope exists for life beyond the grave. The ultimate injustice is that "the wise man dies just like the fool" (cf. 2:14-16). The good and the bad share the same fate in the grave (9:2). When it comes to death, human beings are no better than animals. They both go to dust. Koheleth's thoughts about death bothered him so much that at one point he thought it would be better to be dead (4:2).

The rather contradictory Teacher goes on to say that life is better than death. He repeatedly urges his readers to enjoy life (cf. 2:24; 3:12, 22; 5:18; 8:15; 9:7-9 11:7-10). Listen to Koheleth's recommendation. "So I commend enjoyment, for there is nothing better for people under the sun than to eat, and drink, and enjoy themselves, for this will go with them in their toil through the days of life that God gives them under the sun" (8:15). Koheleth suggests a little enjoyment before life ends with death.

Koheleth helps us think about life's injustices and the projection of God's justice. Koheleth saw various injustices taking place "under the sun." He saw injustice in the law courts (3:6-12) and in the marketplace (4:1-3). While the mistreatment of the weak displeased him, he calls for no social reforms such as we find in the Prophets (cf. Amos 5:21-24). He seems to accept injustice as a sad fact of life but one that deeply disturbs him. He calls for readers to "look, the tears of the oppressed." What troubles Koheleth is the absence of apparent divine response to the suffering. The Teacher is also concerned with the power of the oppressor. The misuse of power and the lack of concern for the oppressed brought Koheleth to despair. He concluded that death was better than life (4:2), and it was better to have never been born than to witness a world of despair.

Koheleth believes, or at least tries to believe, that God will eventually execute justice (cf. 3:17; 11:9b). In the epilogue the narrator makes a conclusion when he says, "For God will bring every deed into judgment including every secret thing, whether good or evil" (12:14). Koheleth's references to divine judgment are not something new. He mentioned it in 3:17 and 11:9. The Teacher does not describe the judgment. He merely asserts its certainty. James L. Crenshaw notes that divine judgment is a "comforting word for good people but a frightening word for sinners."[21]

Finally, reading Ecclesiastes makes us stop and think of life without God and a life with God. The Teacher did not major on the sins of society. He gave a brief mention of Solomon's concubines, but he did not write extensively on the sensual sins. He did mention more the sins of the temperament such as greed, jealousy, and envy. Koheleth focused primarily on life in secular society. It was a good life of working, playing, studying, marrying, making money, and other activities. He saw nothing wrong with these activities. The problem in Koheleth's thinking is that God is left out in all of these activities. In order words, people do good things without even considering God in their lives. Some writers call this "practical atheism."

Jesus told the story of a successful farmer. His fields yielded a bountiful harvest. It was so much that his present barns had to be replaced with larger barns. He adopted the lifestyle of eating, drinking, and being merry for tomorrow we die. The farmer did nothing morally wrong. There is nothing wrong with being a good farmer. His problem was that he left God out of his life and his future plans.

Koheleth observes secular society. He sees hard work, good investments, educational endeavors, and other activities. But he does not see the society's consciousness of God's existence or presence. Thus, secular society without God becomes empty, meaningless, pessimistic, and absurd.

Koheleth sees a better life when God is considered. He sees God is the absolute and transcendent ruler of the world. He sees that God controls the details of life, but he does keep a distance. Though remote, God gives good things to people. He wants them to enjoy the pleasure possible with his gifts (9:7). Koheleth seeks to open the reader's eyes to the world as he sees it. God has relationship with individuals. Life is better when individuals acknowledge, obey, and believe in God.

Reading and studying Ecclesiastes involves seeing the life situation and the literary uniqueness, and its application to today's world. But more than mere observation the writer of Ecclesiastes wants readers to think. The writer does not coerce, force, or manipulate how a person thinks or lives his or her life. He looks at life with occasional glimpses of God and wants the readers to think, consider, evaluate, ponder, then eventually decide the ultimate meaning of life and choose or not choose a relationship with their Creator.

Chapter 2

A Personal Ventilation about Life

1:2-11

As stated in the previous chapter of this work, the first part of Ecclesiastes contains the words of someone speaking about Koheleth. This second person introduces Koheleth (1:1) and then this wise man summarizes Koheleth's thinking (2-11). The prologue of 1:1-2:11 is the second wise man's introduction prior to encountering the observations and reflections of Koheleth about life. This prologue summarizes the mood for what follows in Koheleth's speeches. He gives a foretaste of the Teacher's conclusion that he reached in his inspections and deliberations of life. The tone of the prologue is somber and expresses the fact that while there is a lot of activity in the world, it is rather tiresome. It could be compared to the world on a treadmill running constantly but never getting anywhere. In this prologue this second wise man summarizes the Teacher so closely that it appears that the narrator's feelings are the same as the Teacher.

An Honest Look at Life: Ecclesiastes

Albert Camus, the French atheistic, existential philosopher, ventilates his philosophy of the meaninglessness of life in his work *The Myth of Sisphus*. According to the Greek myth, the gods condemned Sisphus to roll a large rock to the top of a mountain, only to have the rock roll back down to the bottom every time he reached the top. Sisphus's entire existence is exerted toward accomplishing nothing but rolling the rock. Camus notes the meaninglessness of the process is reflected in the absurd daily lives of people. He concludes that a person finds happiness by rolling his or her rock.

The narrator, or the second wise man, begins Ecclesiastes with Koheleth having a kindred attitude with Albert Camus. Fortunately Camus' philosophy is constant while Koheleth's observations seem to be occasional. If we are honest, all of us find something of despair about life from time to time. We look at life at times and conclude that it does not make sense. We often have our down moments when the universe and our lives seem to have no meaning. Koheleth ventilates his honest feelings about life at a particular time in his existence. He will cautiously propose responses to his ventilation about meaninglessness.

The narrator's report of Koheleth's ventilation began with an utterance about his present pessimistic attitude about life (1:2). His ventilation continues with a thought-provoking question about the profit one gains from life (1:3). Next Koheleth reports about how nature goes on day after day with regular monotony (1:4-7). He further tells how human experience is dull and unsatisfying (1:8). The writer concludes his pessimistic utterance with the observation that history never changes. Nothing new ever happens (1:9-11). Two much honesty blitzes many people. These people want easy answers to life. The narrator hits the readers with Koheleth's absolute honest observations about life. Early reading of Ecclesiastes causes the reader to think the writer views life as purely meaningless.

A Pessimistic Introduction

1:2

The narrator reports how the Teacher does not begin on a positive note about life. Instead, he introduces a major theme of the entire book in 1:2. "Vanity of vanities," says the Teacher, vanity of vanities! All is vanity." This verse is important because it introduces the word *hebel*, a Hebrew word translated "vanity." The word becomes a veritable refrain throughout the book. The word is used thirty-eight times in Ecclesiastes. W. Sibley Towner has the notion that *hebel* forms a literary bracket (1:2-2:28) around the body of the Teacher's work.[1]

Scholars make many interesting proposals about the

precise meaning of *hebel*. The word denotes a vivid image, namely, vapor or breath, while connoting something empty and worthless. Vapor is present only for a brief second, and then it is gone. All things in the world are like vapor. The New Revised Standard Version retains the translation of *hebel* as "vanity," as the King James Version does. Numerous other suggestions have been made for the translation of hebel—"emptiness," "meaninglessness," and "absurdity." *Hebel* or "vanity" is like a mirage in which human efforts, hopes, and plans evaporated and are replaced by want and misery.

Towner thinks "absurdity" conveys the Teacher's meaning across the millennia into contemporary English. Today the word absurdity has come to mean more than a silly, foolish thing. It is that which cannot be understood through any of the rubrics people use to explain the meaning of their experience. Thus, *hebel* is not just "vapor" that disappears. It may in fact go on and on. But it makes no more sense at the end than it did at the beginning. It is the living of life without finding any meaning in it. It is "pushing the rock" up the mountain without any accomplishment.[2]

Absurdity seems to be the conviction that Koheleth holds in his reflections on the meaning of life. Everything is *hebel*. Nothing can be counted on to work out the way it should. Nothing makes any ultimate sense. Various accomplishments can be made. Various experiences produce happiness. However, over against all the Teacher's accomplishments and experiences stands his ventilation, "All is absurd."

The traditional systems by which life could be understood do not work. Pain, loss, failure, and death happen unexpectedly. Correspondence between deed and consequences does not happen. Virtue and reward do not coincide. Vice and punishment do not make sense.

The word *hebel* appears five times in verse 3. When the Hebrews used a word twice in succession, it meant the most that something can be. Thus, the holy of holies is the most holy place and the king of Kings is the most important king. The Teacher repeats "vanity" again and again to make sure the reader gets the point that human existence on earth is like a vapor, vanity.

The narrator thinks Koheleth sees "all" of human life subject to absurdity. He leaves nothing out. He cannot find meaning in any person or thing. What does the Teacher means when he says, "All is vanity?" Does he include godliness or God? If "all" includes those topics, the Teacher would be desperately and profoundly out of harmony with the rest of Old Testament Scripture. He was not a nihilist in the tradition of Albert Camus. But he was a realist. The context of Koheleth's "all" comes in verse 3 when he says plainly that what he has in mind are the things "under the sun." What the narrator reports is rather pessimistically true because he thinks the Teacher focuses primarily on purely earthly values. Each time the phrase "under the sun" appears, he thinks of life from a secular point of view.

A Thought-Provoking Question

1:3

Immediately following his theme of vanity, the narrator projects a question that the Teacher would ask: "What do people gain from all of the toil at which they toil under the sun?" (1:3). Of course the rhetorical question is asked primarily for effect. No answer is expected, and none is needed because the answer seems to be so obvious. People gain nothing from all their labor under the sun. The purpose of the question is to get the readers to think. What is the gain of all the activities in which people participate on the earth?

The narrator becomes dialogical with his readers early in the book. Though the Teacher's question is obvious, the reader must nonetheless think about supplying an answer. The word "gain" (yitron) is a key word in Ecclesiastes. It appears nine times (1:3; 2:11, 13; 3:9; 5:8, 15; 7:12; 10:10–11). The word does not appear anywhere else in the Hebrew Old Testament. The word comes from a verb meaning "to be left over" or "to remain." The word was used to describe the gain accruing from a business deal.

The narrator reports that the Teacher observes life being typified by toilsome activity. Generations come and go, the sun rises and sets, the wind blows incessantly in its circuitous courses, and streams flow constantly without ever filling the sea (1:4–7). The whole earth is a scene of incessant activity and movement. With all the constant activity taking place, one would think that something is being accomplished. Yet, even as the years go by, any semblance of progress is only a mirage.

The implication of Koheleth's thought-provoking question is more evident in his use of the phrase "under the sun." The phrase occurs twenty-nine times in Ecclesiastes. It appears nowhere else in the Hebrew Bible than Ecclesiastes. By the phrase the Teacher thinks of the common experiences of human beings on the earth. It is a look at life from the human perspective. It means a secular world. An "under the sun" existence is a lifestyle purely based on this earth without consideration for God.

Koheleth's use of the phrase "under the sun" highlights the restricted scope of his ventilation. He limited his feelings to human life on earth. If one's view of life goes no further than life "under the sun," all of our endeavors will be like pushing a rock up the hill only to have to go back to the bottom. If human resources and experiences are entirely of this world, the answer of "no gain" would be obvious. There is another realm that the Teacher will mention later when he speaks of God. Meanwhile, the reader must be patient with Koheleth and hear his ventilations about life "under the sun." Preoccupation with only an earthly existence does lead to the ventilation of pessimism.

Koheleth's question causes us to think: While life "under the sun" may be enjoyable and somewhat fulfilling, can it bring ultimate joy and fulfillment to life? Koheleth's question needs to be asked by every generation because emptiness brought by earthly existence prompts the question, Is this all there is to life?

A Monotonous Succession

1:4-7

The narrator continues Koheleth's ventilation that nothing is profitable and that all things are pointless in verses 4-7. The writer looks at creation for evidence. He looks at nature's cycle as evidence that nothing really changes. Everything goes in one continuous circle. Generations follow generations but the earth remains constant. Koheleth's frustration is agitated between the brevity of human life and the permanence of earthly creation.

What can be more vain or absurd than humans passing off the scene of earth and the earth remaining? Humans, who were created to have dominion, dissolve into the dust while the earth keeps on going. "A generation goes, and a generation comes, but the earth remains forever" (1:4). The writer could have been looking across the mountains. He saw the mountains' massiveness that had been there for so long. Numerous generations had seen them. He pondered the depths of the sea and the changelessness of the desert sand. Then he compared the creation to human beings. Humans come and go so quickly. Human life is fleeting, transient, precarious, and disposable.

The word "generation" is related to a Hebrew verb that denotes circular movement.[3] The noun has traditionally been understood to mean "generation." What the Teacher does is contrast the permanence of humans over the impermanence of the inanimate world.[4] The participles "goes" and "comes" imply continuity of action. The writer depicts a human generation going and a human generation coming.

The writer makes a notable transition: "But the earth remains forever." He presents a striking contrast of the impermanence of human generations to the permanence of nature. The terms "goes" and "comes" in verse 4 establish a motif that unites verses 4–7. Three examples are given for the monotonous repetition of nature: the repetitious cycle of the sea; the wind blowing round the circuits with no apparent purpose; and the water running into the sea without ever finding the task accomplished.

The images of sun, wind, and rivers in verse 4–7 convey the theme of busyness without any meaning. "The sun rises and the sun goes down, and hurries to the place where it rises" (1:5). The Teacher observes the continuous rising and setting of the sun. The pattern remains the same day after day and year after year. The idea of continuous, repetitive action seems to be the emphasis of verse 5. The word "hurries" comes from a Hebrew verb which means "to gasp, pant." It depicts the sun as a weary runner breathing heavily in a race. The repeated words "rises," "goes down," and "hurries" communicate monotony.

The second illustration from nature is the wind. "The wind blows to the south, and goes around to the north; round and round goes the wind and on its circuits the wind returns" (1:6). Once again the idea of sameness without apparent change is noted. The wind has lots of action, but when examined closely, it is just going in circles. The action of the wind evokes the idea of a lot of action with little consequences. James Crenshaw notes that the use of repetitive participles "goes" and "going around" gives a sense of being caught in a rut.[5]

The writer's final illustration pictures water or rivers going into the sea. "All streams run to the sea, but the sea is not full; to the place where the streams flow, there they continue to flow" (1:7). The streams have ceaseless activity but no change. Things appear to be changing, but in reality they remain the same.

Next, the narrator reports how Koheleth observes that the streams, which flow consistently into the sea, do not affect the level of the sea. The verbs in verse 7 graphically depict the repetition found in the other illustrations—"run," "flow." The Teacher observes the great activity of the steams but little or no change in the sea.

According to the narrator, creation from Koheleth's vantage point lacks any sense of grand design. To him sun, wind, and streams represent objects locked in perpetual motion. And so it is also, Koheleth contends, with human beings. Like the wind that blows "round and round," human beings find themselves "chasing after wind." As the waters flow in vain to fill the sea, so human beings strive to no avail to fulfill their hopes and desires. The created order for Koheleth proves to be the reflection of humankind's foil in the quest for meaningful existence.

The sun, wind, and streams mirror human experiences. The monotony of lives condemned to repetition cause many to despair of life. Novelty seems to offer the only escape. So people change jobs, move to other places, enter another career, buy gadgets, and leave wives or husbands to get another spouse. If outward changes do not work, they make mental shifts. Their career, in which they have invested so much, becomes peripheral. They invest their thinking in another cause or a hobby for a time until that, too, loses its attraction. In the end it makes little difference. Daily life is still the prime reality which must be faced. And that is a repetitious nightmare.[6]

A Continuous Dissatisfaction

1:8

The second wise man reports that Koheleth takes his ventilations a step further. Despite the fact that creation is active to the point of inexpressible exhaustion, it does not provide human beings with any lasting satisfaction. Despite what appears to be constant change, it is really only an illusion. There is no rest for the sun, the wind, or the streams. Only ceaseless toil and endless work occur that seem to accomplish nothing. This to the Teacher is *hebel*—meaninglessness, vanity, absurdity.

The thought of the ceaseless routine causes the Teacher to ventilate his deepest feelings. "All things are wearisome; more that one can express; the eye is not satisfied with seeing, or the ear filled with hearing" (1:8). The ongoing process of nature without accomplishment leaves the Teacher discouraged and dissatisfied beyond words. The Teacher's pessimism involves comparing the human situation with the cycles of nature. Derek Kidner writes, "Like an ocean, our senses are fed and fed, but never filled. ... The journey goes on; we never arrive."[7]

The expression "all things" could be translated "all words." This translation would stress that the dissatisfaction of human beings is beyond words. The word "wearisome" reflects the Teacher's negative mood both to the endless activity of nature and the fatigue generated by the attempt to comprehend and express what he sees in the world.

Just as the appetite for earthly possessions is never satisfied by amassing goods, so is the human desire for understanding is never satisfied by sensory data. "More than one can express" is a person not able to speak. The weariness of all things is so mind boggling that it exceeds human ability to describe it.[8] The last two clauses explain what things are so wearisome. It is beyond humans to have a sense of satisfaction that leads to closure. Eyes may see much and ears may hear constantly, but it is never enough; there is always more to hear and to see.[9]

No one can speak meaningfully about the world. No one can explain, influence, or control it. However plentiful, words only add to the weight of weariness. The eye also never reaches the point it cannot take in more. We are always looking and listening for that which can bring us satisfaction. Every day we see and hear of endless processions of appeals: YouTube, Facebook, Twitter, BlackBerry, Netflix. We listen to endless streams of sound: iPhone, iPod, iTunes, CDs, and mp3s. Yet, with all the looking and listening, our eyes and ears do not seem to be satisfied. We can never get enough. Like the sea that is never full, the eye is never satisfied with seeing or the ear filled with hearing.

An Unchanging Repetition

1:9-11

The frame narrator next reports how Koheleth turns to history. He notes its futility bears a resemblance to the futility of the created order. History is going nowhere. History—like the sun, wind, and streams—appears to change, but in actuality history remains the same. Nothing new ever happens.

The Hebrew's view of history as expressed in the historical and prophetic books had a cyclic nature, but it was mainly involved progression. Their view of history may be described as a linear, spiral progression but not a meaningless cycle. Over against the normative Old Testament view stands Koheleth saying that the past will perpetually repeat itself in the future. "What has been is what will be, and what has been done is what will be done; there is nothing new under the sun" (1:9). These words are rhythmic heightening the idea of the cyclic repetition of human history.

The Hebrews believed that history is controlled by God. Redemption consists of acts of God in history. Revelation involves authorized interpreters to explain and predict God's acts. History, according to the Old Testament writers, moves toward a goal, namely the day of the Lord. It will be a time when God completes his purpose, redeems his people, and judges his enemies. Koheleth sees that the past (what has been) or human endeavors (what has been done) will change. Gerhard Von Rad thinks the Teacher capitulated to secular philosophy at this point.[10] The Teacher limits his observation and interpretation to the earthly realm. The rest of the Old Testament stresses that God acts in new ways even on the earth.

History's cyclic nature , according to Koheleth, is expressed with, "There is nothing new under the sun." It has already been done in the past. The expression underscores the writer's cyclic view of history. Readers will have to wait for Koheleth's more optimistic view about God's justice in the future. Also, they will have to wait for the pronounced linear view of history where biblical writers spoke of history moving toward a victorious end with God.

In verse 10 the Teacher anticipates an objection to the claim that there is nothing new under the sun. "Is this a thing of which it is said, 'See this is new?'" Koheleth's objection is short and abrupt. "It has already been in the ages before us" (1:10b). For Koheleth history seems to move on in its frenetic inertia, every repetitive and wearisome. No upward on onward movement is attainable, regardless of how much energy is expended. Houses are built only to crumble and to be built again. There is no war to end all wars. Generations come and go, and the wheel is always reinvented. Newness to Koheleth is an illusion.

The Teacher concludes his ventilation with the assertion that human beings' most noble efforts will not be remembered, nor will there be any remembrance of people yet to come by those who come after them (1:11). The Teacher pessimistically forecasts that life will always be the same. Present generations think they are engaged in memorable moments, but the next generation will not care and may not have heard anything about the present generation or their works. Past events are forgotten; future events will also be forgotten.

Orthodox Hebrews lived in light of former events. Later in Ecclesiastes the Teacher will invite the readers "to remember" our Creator (12:1) and to keep in mind what lies ahead (11:8). On secular premises the past, the present, and the future have no meaning. Secular man will confirm the maxim, "He who does not learn from history is destined to repeat it."[11]

All throughout verses 2-11 the narrator has reported Koheth's thinking to be restricted to a life "under the sun" mentality. He has limited his observations to the earthly realm. Neither creation nor history makes sense from a secularist viewpoint. The Teacher in 1:2-11 thinks of life from a purely horizontal viewpoint.

The author's ventilation causes reader to think. Is there anything beyond the sun which could change the pessimistic perspective? Is there a reality that would help us see that life consists of more than rolling the rock? Is there a transcendent dimension that would help us? The Teacher has been ventilating that secularism can only produce a life which is profoundly unsatisfying. Life "under the sun" produces emptiness, monotony, vanity, boredom, absurdity, and pessimism. Perhaps something or Someone above the sun could cause life on earth to be different.

Chapter 3

An Autobiography of an Illustrious Life

1:12–2:26

After introducing the Teacher and what he thinks of life by a narrator, Koheleth then proceeds to introduce himself. Readers of Ecclesiastes notice a literary change beginning in 1:12. Koheleth himself speaks for the first time. He continues in the first person until there is a change to the third person in 12:8. His observations of life and his wisdom admonitions constitute the main body of the book. From the standpoint of chronology, 1:12 could be the beginning of the book, and all that precedes could be considered prologue (1:1–11).

The entire unit of 1:12–2:26 appears in the form of an autobiographical narrative. Notice the personal references in the section: "I, the Teacher," (1:12a), "I applied my mind," (1:13a), "I have seen everything," (1:14a), "I said to myself," (2:1a), " I will make a test," (2:1b), "So I turned to consider," (2:12), "I searched with my mind," (2:3), "So I turned to consider," (2:12), "This also I saw,"(2:24b). This unit consists of an introduction presenting the speaker, his station, his qualities, and the task he set for himself. Specifically, Koheleth introduces himself and describes the task he took upon himself: to use wisdom to gain an understanding of the world.[1]

In this unit the Teacher writes as if he were Solomon, the wise and wealthy king of Israel. In 1:1 he identifies himself as "the Teacher, the son of David, king in Jerusalem." The Teacher probably wrote Ecclesiastes hundreds of years after Solomon's death. But in this unit the writer pretends to be Solomon in order to give his important message greater impact. Such a technique resembles a tradition of Near Eastern wisdom literature, especially Egyptian and Phoenician. An old man claims to be a king and draws from the lifetime of another king to give advice to his son or successor.

Koheleth made the choice of "royal fiction" because Solomon was the archetypical wise king but also in view of his great wealth and reputation. If Solomon, who possessed everything a person could possess, found all his effort to find fulfillment profoundly unsatisfying, how much more would lesser persons be likely to fail in that attempt. The speaker never says that he is Solomon, but the reader from the context can clearly identify Solomon in 1:12–2:26. Some contemporary preachers follow a similar device in the "dramatic monologue" sermon. In this technique the preacher assumes the character of a Bible person, and the preacher gets the point across by speaking as if he were really that Bible person.

Of course those who hold to Solomon as the author of Ecclesiastes generally believe that Solomon wrote Ecclesiastes in his old age and speaks from the vantage point of an old man looking back on life. Therefore, those who hold this view think Solomon tells his own autobiography in 1:12-2:26. Whatever view one holds about the actual author of Ecclesiastes, two truths are clear whatever one believes about who wrote the book. First, the truth is the same whether Solomon tells his own story or another author tells Solomon's story as if he were Solomon. Second, the circumstances fit the life of Solomon irrespective of the author.

Solomon had the reputation of great wealth. He had numerous pleasures at his disposal. Traditionally, Solomon represents the possession of wisdom. A person with such an illustrious life as Solomon seems to be a wonderful example of a person's search for the meaning of life. He had abundant opportunities to discover whether wealth, wisdom, achievements, pleasure, or sexual exploits would bring lasting pleasure and satisfaction. In this writer's opinion the study of 1:12-2:26 involves personal insights from the Teacher as if he were Solomon. Every movement in this unit uses the first-personal pronoun for an autobiographical purpose. The speaker in 1:12–2:26 takes upon himself to use human wisdom to gain understanding of the world. As the unit progresses and concludes, the Teacher states his conclusion: everything is "vanity and a chasing after the wind." Notice the progression in the writer's pilgrimage through life.

Personal Reflections

1:12-18

The text begins in the pattern of an autobiographical introduction much like the ones found in other Near Eastern writings. The language and style of Koheleth's self-introduction are drawn from Egyptian and Phoenician inscriptions, which typically boast of a king's reputation and accomplishments. Koheleth departs from the pattern of boasting and turns the royal testimony into a confession of failure. Such identifications as the Phoenicians, Egyptians, and the one in Ecclesiastes introduce autobiographical accounts of past kings and their lives. Examples from Phoenician inscriptions are: "I am Kilamuwa, the son of Hayya"; "I am Azitawadda, blessed by Baal, servant of Baal, whom Awarku, king of the Danunians, made powerful."[2]

Obviously, the text introduces Solomon. "I, the Teacher,

when king over Jerusalem" (1:12). The phrase "king over Jerusalem" resembles the comment found in 1:1 "the son of David, king in Jerusalem." These references speak of Solomon whether from his own pen or from "royal fiction." This description only fits the life of Solomon because, although Rehoboam and other descendants of David ruled in Jerusalem, none of them ruled over Israel. After Solomon the kingdom divided between Israel and Judah, and whoever was king in Jerusalem only ruled over the southern kingdom of Judah, not over the northern kingdom of Israel.

The autobiography actually begins in 1:13 where the writer presents an account of his quest for understanding. "And I applied my mind to seek and to search out by wisdom all that is done under heaven" (1:13a). After introducing himself in 1:12, Koheleth describes his personal search for meaning in life. This part of the unit may be divided into two parts of reflection: the first in verses 13–15 and the second in verses 16–18. Each part concludes with a proverb. The first reflection describes the intense actions of his search, and the second reflection reports the failure of his search.

The Teacher tells about his intense search for life's meaning: "I applied my mind." His search was earnest and sincere. The word "mind" denotes his inner life, the center of his mental, emotional, and spiritual capacities. The thoroughness of his search may be seen in the verbs "seek" and "search." The first verb means to look deeply into something, and the latter verb means to search thoroughly over a wide area. The scope of the Teacher's investigation was incredibly intense: "all that is done under heaven." Solomon was renowned by wisdom, wealth, achievements, and women. He had abundant opportunity to discover whether these life experiences brought lasting pleasure and satisfaction. Wisdom was the Teacher's primary method of investigation and reflection. He wanted to understand all the world's phenomena. He aims at nothing less than to understand the totality of human existence.

In the latter part of verse 13 and in verse 14, the Teacher offers a summary of his search. He gives his first reflection on his search for life's meaning. "It is an unhappy business that God has given to human beings to be busy with" (1:13b). Koheleth reflects on his search for life's meaning using human wisdom. First, he concludes that the search is an "unhappy business." The pursuit of life from a secular perspective turns out to be an unhappy pursuit. The longer people look for answers "under the sun," the harder they find life not understandable or satisfying. Koheleth sees the search for understanding from the world's perspective to be a hopeless, frustrating task.

A second conclusion from the Teacher of his search for

life's meaning involves "a vanity and a chasing after the wind." Humans desire a sense of gain or profit in life and satisfaction in the world around them, but these traits elude them as they experience life. "I saw all the deeds that are done under the sun; and see, all is vanity and a chasing after the wind" (1:14). This verse reflects the lament of searching for satisfaction in mere earthly existence. The Teacher faces problems he cannot solve and experiences hardships without a sense of hope. What a graphic expression the Teacher uses to describe his pursuit for life's meaning from a purely secularistic pursuit—"chasing after the wind." The expression pictures emptiness of life lived only from the pursuit of earthly adventures.

The third summary statement about the Teacher's search comes in the form of a proverb: "What is crooked cannot be made straight, and what is lacking cannot be counted" (1:15). Twists (crooked) and gaps (what is lacking) are part of all of human reasoning and searching. No matter how much the thinker ponders, he cannot straighten life's anomalies or reduce all of what he sees to a neat formula. The Teacher repeats the age-old problem of the wise men of the ancient Near East. They were aware of their finitude and their inability to discover unaided the truths about life. The Teacher's wisdom may help in some things, but it cannot solve the basic problems of life.

Koheleth moves from one reflection recorded in verses 13-15 to another reflection about his search in verses 16-18. He begins with a personal introduction. "I said to myself, 'I have acquired great wisdom, surpassing all who were in Jerusalem before me, and my mind has had great experiences of wisdom and knowledge'" (1:16). Koheleth presents his credentials. He may sound rather presumptuous in his claims for unsurpassed wisdom, but that is not the point he wishes to make. His point is, if he cannot find meaning in or through wisdom, then who can? His attempt to solve the problem of life by human understanding also enhanced the problem. As long as wisdom is restricted to the realm "under the sun" the pursuit fails to bring satisfaction. The Teacher's use of the synonyms "wisdom" and "knowledge" seems to make his reflection more emphatic.[3]

Koheleth again reflects his search for life's meaning and reflects on the search. "And I applied my mind to know wisdom and to know madness and folly" (1:17a). The Teacher does not give up. He continues to search for meaning. After his first attempt ended in failure, he had a heart-to-heart talk within himself and decided to continue the pursuit. Koheleth tells us he pursed wisdom, madness, and folly. Evidently, he thought he could understand life's meaning by studying opposites. He wants to know precisely how wisdom differs from madness and folly. He wants the picture of life from both sides. The comparison only led to "striving after the wind" (1:17b).

The second reflection of the Teacher concludes like the first reflection with a proverb: "For in such wisdom is much vexation, and those who increase knowledge increase sorrow" (1:18). The more he explores, the greater his perplexity. Robert Davidson writes, "In the end, he is left facing a mystery which he is no more nearer solving than that he set out. For all his knowledge, he is no nearer discovering the ultimate meaning of life."[4]

Koheleth has shared two reflections about his search for life's meaning by human wisdom. Both reflections end in meaningless frustration: "vanity" and "chasing after wind." Readers of Ecclesiastes have unique access to Solomon's personal diary, which records his personal reflections. Readers learn of Solomon's search for meaning by human wisdom. In two places Solomon emphasized the failure of human wisdom to produce satisfaction. Koheleth turns from personal reflection to personal experiences, which were supposed to produce satisfaction. Wisdom and knowledge increase a person's awareness of the inequities and absurdities of life without giving the ability to remedy them.

Personal Experiences

2:1-12

Koheleth now turns to personal experiences in the life of Solomon. Having failed to find meaning in searching out wisdom, he decides to share his personal experiences in life. He first tells about his pursuit of pleasure. "I said to myself, 'Come now, I will make a test of pleasure; enjoy yourself.' But again, this was also vanity. I said of laughter, 'It is mad,' and of pleasure, 'What use is it?'" (2:1-2). The expression "I said to myself" again reflects the author's self-talk. He made an intentional effort to enjoy life with abundant pleasures.

In Ecclesiastes the word "pleasure" does not suggest immoral action. In fact in 2:26 the Teacher calls pleasure a gift of God. The problem is that the Teacher seeks to find meaning in pleasure "under the sun." In other words, he sought pleasure that only earthly existence offers. He does not take God into consideration in his pleasures. He quickly concludes that the pursuit of pleasure on earth is futile.

Koheleth specifies two areas of enjoyment: "laughter" and "pleasure." "Laughter" seems to relate to superficial enjoyment. It was used of the fun enjoyed during a game or a party. The game ends and the party is over, and then the laughter ceases. The word "pleasure" means more thoughtful joy. The two enjoyments receive similar verdicts. Laughter is mad, and pleasure is profitless. All pleasures, whatever their nuances, fail to meet the needs of humans whose horizons remain on an earthly existence.

The Teacher goes into great detail about his personal experiences. First, he tells of his experience with alcohol. "I searched with my mind how to cheer my body with wine—my mind still guiding me with wisdom—and how to lay hold on folly, till I might see what was good for the sons of men to do under heaven during that few days of their life" (2:3). Alcohol is a popular way to find cheer in life or to escape life's troubles.

The Teacher found wine was a lubricant for his laughter. This experience has been difficult to interpret. To "cheer my body with wine" strikes a somewhat negative note. One the surface one could think the Teacher abused alcohol in an addictive manner. Some scholars think the Teacher was not being controlled by wine but his "mind [was] still guiding" him with wisdom. He was not given over to drunken debauchery but drinking in moderation and thoughtfully assessing his experience. He used wine to enhance his enjoyments of life. Evidently the wine did not give him insight into what is good for people during their brief stay on earth, for the Teacher moves quickly to another experience.

The Teacher shifts from purely sensual and self-centered pleasures to the more grandiose achievements of human endeavor. "I made great works; I built houses and planted vineyards for myself. I made myself gardens and parks and planted in them all kinds of fruit trees. I made myself pools from which to water the forest of growing trees. I bought male and female slaves, and had slaves who were born in my house" (2:4-7a). "I made great works" introduces a number of Koheleth's accomplishments. Temper Longman III writes, "Here we see the usefulness of the fictional associational with Solomon."[5] The historical book of 1 Kings has an account of Solomon's great building projects and vineyards. If Solomon could find no significance in building accomplishments, who could?

Notice the purpose in building the great buildings and planting the large vineyards. The continuous use of "for myself" indicates Solomon's preoccupation with himself. His purpose was to plant and to build in order to satisfy himself, not to help other people.

Because of the size of the building projects, Solomon needed a large workforce to build and maintain these projects. He purchased many slaves, and the slaves had children who also belonged to the master's house. To feed all his slaves, he had to keep flocks of cattle and herds of sheep and goats all over his property.

The Teacher continues to relate Solomon's experiences with sensual pleasures. He tells of Solomon's great wealth. "I also gathered for myself silver and gold and the treasure of kings and provinces" (2:8a). Solomon's treasure was large because of the product of foreign tribute (treasure of kings) and of people's taxation (provinces). The book of 1 Kings mentions Solomon's gold and silver reserves (1 Kings 10:14–25).

The Teacher tells how Solomon added the pleasure of art. "I got singers, both men and women" (2:8b). Music was a rare pleasure in Solomon's day, but Solomon could afford to bring it into his palace, engaging entire choirs to sing.

Next, Koheleth describes Solomon's sexual pleasures. "I got . . . many concubines, man's delight" (2:8c). The Ecclesiastes text relates "many concubines," but 1 Kings 11:3 relates that Solomon had seven hundred wives and princesses with three hundred concubines. It was indeed the "Playboy Mansion" of the ancient world. These women afforded Solomon more sexual partners than anyone could imagine. These concubines are called "man's delight," which is a reference to purely erotic, physical pleasure.

The Teacher provides a summary statement to his experiences with sensual pleasures. He lived better and celebrated life harder than anyone around him. "So I became great and surpassed all who were before me in

Jerusalem; also my wisdom remained with me" (2:9). He kept his mind alert during the enjoyment of his pleasures to evaluate possible benefits.

Koheleth clearly states that he exercised no restraint, no self-denial in his pursuit for the meaning in sensual pleasures. "And whatever my eyes desired I did not keep from them; I kept my heart from no pleasure, for my heart found pleasure in my toil" (2:10). Whatever he saw that he wanted, he got it. He did not deny himself anything he wanted.

At this point Koheleth comes to Harold Kushner's conclusion *When Everything You Want Isn't Enough*. Koheleth admits great rewards are gained from sensual pleasures, but the ultimate objects of his search—"profit" and "meaning"—were lacking. "Then I considered all that my hands had done and the toil I had spend it doing it, and behold, all was vanity and a striving after wind, and that was nothing to be gained under the sun" (2:11). Koheleth's summary could be the answer to his rhetorical question in 1:3, "What do people gain from all the toil at which they toil under the sun?" This answer is nothing. All the Teacher's key terms combine with this conclusion—toil, vanity, striving after wind, nothing to be gained under the sun. These terms convey bitter disillusionment. Materialism, hedonism, and consumerism fail to provide human beings with meaning.

An Honest Look at Life: Ecclesiastes
Personal Contemplation
2:12-23

In all of Koheleth's sensual pleasure, he never lost the power of rational thinking. Oftentimes materialism and hedonism steal the logical thinking process of human beings. But Koheleth never "lost his mind" in his many pursuits. He moves from relating his personal experiences to relating his rational thinking or his personal contemplation. In this section he looks back on life and does some serious thinking.

Koheleth shares his contemplation about wisdom in 2:12-14a. Earlier in his life he thought the pursuit of wisdom would give him the answers to the questions of life (1:12-15). But there were so many things in life he could not straighten out. Information failed to produce transformation. With a typical phrase, "I turned my attention," Koheleth changes the subject. He turns to the topic of wisdom and folly. "So I turned to consider wisdom and madness and folly; for what can the man do who comes after the king? Only what he has already done" (2:12). Whether the person is Solomon or Solomon's ghostwriter, the Teacher loved to say that Solomon's successor could not improve on his wisdom. If he cannot find the meaning of life, then who can?

The Teacher discerns a major difference between a wise

person and a fool. "Then I saw that wisdom exceeds folly as light excels darkness" (2:13). Yes, Koheleth still has his wit. He praises the value of wisdom. It is much better than folly. He expresses the contrast between wisdom and folly with the terms of light and darkness. It is better to be in the light than in the dark. The Teacher expands his comparison by saying, "The wise man has his eyes in his head, but the fool walks in darkness" (2:14a). Wise people walk with a clear head in a well-lit room. Fools walk as if they are blind. Wise people navigate life better, but the fool keeps stumbling over obstacles.

After this striking comparison of wisdom and folly, the Teacher introduces a surprising reversal. He introduces the idea of a common fate of both the wise and the fool. "And yet I perceived that one fate comes to all of them" (2:14b). That fate is death, and it comes to the wise and fool alike. Koheleth's contemplation prompts the question, What is the profit of being so wise? If the wise as well as the fool end up dead, there seem to be no gain in being wise.

When Koheleth contemplated his mortality, he talked to himself in the privacy of his soul. "Then I said to myself, 'What happens to the fool will happen to me also; so then why have I been so very wise?' And I said to myself that this also is vanity" (2:15). He comes to doubt the whole wisdom enterprise. He concludes with the reflection that wisdom is meaningless, absurd. His reason for assessing wisdom as absurd is because of the inevitability of death.

Koheleth becomes frustrated in his contemplation about death. Ultimately he will die, and his memory will pass from the earth. "For there is no enduring remembrance of the wise or of fools, seeing that in the days to come all will have been long forgotten. How can the wise did just like fools?" (22:16). The wise person will die and will be forgotten, and this reality renders the Teacher's pursuit of wisdom insignificant to him.

The Teacher comes to a tragic conclusion after his contemplation about wisdom. "So I hated life, because what is done under the sun was grievous to me; for all is vanity and a chasing after wind" (2:17). The Teacher hated life because of the inevitability of death and the absurdity of losing all his wisdom as a result of death. As long as one looks at life from an "under the sun" perspective, he will hate life.

Koheleth moves away from personal contemplation about the worth of wisdom to personal contemplation about the worth of work (2:18–23). He thinks about the satisfaction toil or work should have brought him. "I hated all my toil in which I have toiled under the sun, seeing that I must leave it to those who whom after me—and who know whether they will be wise or foolish? Yet they will be master of all for which I toiled and used my wisdom under the sun. This also is vanity"(2:18-19). The Teacher hates his work. He expected work to give him a sense of meaning and purpose in life. Two problems were associated with his work. The first problem was that after our death someone else will profit from our hard work. Perhaps our possessions will end up in good hands, or again perhaps they will not. Oddly enough, when Solomon died, his earnings went to his oldest son Rehoboam. This son was so foolish that he lost a large portion of his father's kingdom.

As a result of Koheleth's contemplation about his wealth going to a fool, he slipped into depression. "So I turned and gave my heart up to despair concerning all the toil of my labors under the sun, because sometimes one who has toiled with wisdom and knowledge and skill must leave all to be enjoyed by another who did not toil for it. This also is vanity and a great evil" (2:20-21). The Teacher hated his toil, seeing that he must leave it to those who came after him. Who knows whether the person coming after him will be wise or foolish? He will be the master of all for which he had toiled and used his wisdom. This has to be vanity, absurd. It was enough to drive the Teacher into depression.

The second problem with Koheleth's work was its weariness and trouble. "What do mortals get from all the toil and strain with which they toil under the sun? For all their days are full of pain, and their work is a vexation; even at night their minds do no rest. This also is vanity" (2:22-23). The Teacher concludes that all of his work was not worth the effort. Koheleth asks a question, "What is the profit of gain of work?" The Teacher answers his own question about work in verse 22. He gives two insights. First, people work hard throughout the day, and their effort is filled with heavy physical and mental exhaustion. Second, at night they could replenish their resources with rest, but their mental thoughts do not stop. His conclusion is a familiar one, "This also is vanity."

Well, the Teacher using the illustrious life of Solomon has brought us to an apparent dead end. He has failed with his experiments with wealth, pleasure, achievements, and sex. He found no meaning in seeking to learn life by wisdom. He found no genuine happiness in pursuing pleasure. He saw no advantage in being wise in contrast to the fool because both of them die. He saw no lasting benefits from getting possessions for the world's effort in acquiring wealth, for at death no one knows who will get the possessions that are left. He asks, "Is there any benefit to living life on earth?" Oddly enough the Teacher turns from a pessimistic attitude and closes his autobiography on a more positive attitude in 2:24-26.

Personal Solution

2:24–26

Up to Ecclesiastes 2:24 the reader has encountered a rather depressing book. The Teacher's entertainment, work, wisdom, wealth, and pleasure have been declared absurd or meaningless. A surprise surfaces at the close of the autobiography. After two chapters where he has reported the meaninglessness of life, he turns to three verses dealing with meaning. Repeatedly the Teacher has given observations that life "under the sun" is only vanity or meaningless. Out of nowhere the Teacher provides another personal solution to life.

Ecclesiastes 2:24–26 is the first of six passages that allow for the possible enjoyment of life (3:12–14; 3:22; 5:18–20; 8:15; 9:7–10). This is the first passage in which the Teacher gives a partial solution to the problem of living in the world where life seems to be vanity. By anyone's interpretation these texts give a burst of enjoyment for a person who most of the time seemed to be pessimistic.

Take a close look at the Teacher's enjoyment passage. "There is nothing better for mortals than to eat and drink, and find enjoyment in their toil. This also, I saw, is from the hand of God; for apart from him who can eat or who can have enjoyment? For to the one who pleases him God gives wisdom and knowledge and joy; but to the sinner he gives the work of gathering and heaping, only to give to one who pleases God. This also is vanity and a chasing after wind" (2:24–26). Notice the "nothing better" phrase. It appears frequently as Koheleth looks at life and makes evaluations. The phrase simply implies that there is nothing better than what he is recommending in this brief life under the sun. Nothing better exists in this present earthly existence than to eat, drink, and enjoy life.

The Teacher sums up the better way of living with three activities: eat, drink, and find enjoyment in toil. By eating and drinking, he apparently means the common activities of daily life. Even though Koheleth thinks of toil as exhausting and painful (2:22), he nonetheless finds enjoyment in work. He is not advocating a life of sensual pleasure and hedonistic excesses. He has experienced that life and found it unfulfilling (2:1–11). He does not mean pleasure as the goal of life. Instead, he has learned to pursue the simple life, enjoying the ordinary routines of life.[6] Such an attitude toward life has been given a motto after Koheleth wrote: *carpe diem*, a Latin phrase that means "seize the day." Get all the enjoyment out of life that is possible in the present.[7]

Koheleth believes these simple pleasures come from the hand of God. God himself gives the wisdom and knowledge to gain wealth and the ability to find enjoyment in it. The Teacher agrees with orthodox Judaism, which taught that a gracious God is the giver of every gift and that we ought to enjoy these gifts with gratitude. God made human beings to find pleasure in the things he created. What makes the difference in meaninglessness and meaning in life? God makes the difference. Up to this point in Ecclesiastes, God has scarcely been mentioned. But now God's presence seems to make all the difference. According to verse 25, no one can find any true joy in anything apart from God.

The Teacher comes to a prominent stylistic quality in his writing, the rhetorical question. Such questions promote dialogue with the reader. Notice the question: "For apart from him, who can eat or have any other enjoyment?" (2:25). With this question the Teacher sees two kinds of people: the one who pleases God and the one who rebels against God. "For to the one who pleases him God gives wisdom and knowledge and joy; but to the sinner he gives the work of gathering and heaping, only to give to one who pleases God. This also is vanity and a chasing after wind" (2:26). This seems a lot like "good things happen to good people while bad things happed to bad people." Some see this as arbitrary and capricious: God rewards some people and punishes others. No, what the Teacher means is an obvious distinction between people who live under the mercy of God and people who persist in their rebellion against God. The good news is that God gives wisdom, knowledge, and joy to those who seek to do his will. But those who reject God's will continue to flounder as they fruitlessly strive for meaning and purpose, all the while looking in the wrong place. The sinner's pursuit represents "a vanity and a chasing after wind."

In his autobiography, the Teacher has presented two ways of living. On one hand, he has reported the vicious circle of a pointless world filled with temporary pleasures, fruitless work, futile wisdom, and inevitable death. On the other hand, he has reported an enjoyable life taken each day from the hand of God. The Teacher makes no plea, no invitation. He gives a powerful contrast and trusts readers with the awesome decision of what kind of person they want to be.

Chapter 4

An Observation of an Ordered Universe

3:1-15

The Teacher continues to look at life. He has been rather pessimistic in his observations recorded in 1:2-2:23. He has seen life filled with apparent senseless repetitions of natural occurrences (1:2-11). He has experienced life with abundant pleasures, massive wealth, endless entertainment, and engaging work. None of his observations or experiences afforded him fulfillment. It was enough to cause some people to stop searching for life's meaning and to surrender to despair. But not Koheleth, for he never gives up on looking at life.

Koheleth makes a transition in his observation of life. His next insight has more promise than pessimism. He reports what he had observed about time in 3:1-15. He saw that the consistent passing of time gave evidence of a structured universe. He did not see the cosmos characterized by chaos but by order, design, control, and system. The Teacher's report in 3:1-15 stands out as a poetic gem in a seemingly dark and convoluted book.

Michael Eaton thinks Ecclesiastes 3:1–15 elucidates the worldview underlying the life portrayed in 2:24–26. Just as 1:2–2:23 moved from the pessimistic worldview in 1:2–11 to the pessimistic daily life in 1:12–2:23, so in a chiastic movement the thought of 2:24–26 proceeds from the believer's life to the believer's world view in 3:1–15.[1] There is a time for everything The thesis statement of this section is 3:1: "For everything there is a season, and a time for every matter under heaven." This orderliness has to be a great truth. Think of the terrible confusion if the time to plant sometimes fell in July but in other years it was December of February. Koheleth subtly lets his readers know that a Designer and a Sustainer is in control of the affairs of the universe. The regularity and faithfulness of the laws of nature make human existence both livable and, to a great extent, predictable.

Koheleth's record of his observation of an ordered universe centers on the word "time." The Teacher uses the word twenty-eight times distributed over fourteen lines, seven sets each with two pair of opposites. In Jewish thinking the number seven symbolized completeness. Maybe the Teacher intends to depict the complete number of different times humans may encounter in their lifetime.

The Teacher does not intentionally give divisions or points in his reportings. He is much more inductive than deductive. His one idea in 3:1-15 is that God is in control of time and that control makes the cosmos orderly. Ecclesiastes 3:1-15 is the world's most famous poem on the subject of time. More people quote from this chapter than any other one in Ecclesiastes. The folk singer Pete Seeger set the verses to music in the 1950s with a tune the Byrds popularized a decade later in their hit single "Turn, Turn, Turn." But long before the Byrds, the Teacher has struck a responsive chord in human hearts. Though the Teacher does not intentionally divide his theme on time into parts, three noticeable movements emerge: the systematic passing of time, 3:1-8; the sovereign control of time, 3:9-11; and the satisfying experiences within time, 3:12-15.

The Systematic Passing of Time

3:1-8

The Teacher begins his memorable poem with a statement that everything and every activity on earth has its appropriate time. "For everything there is a season, and a time for every matter under heaven" (3:1). Old Testament writers commonly saw purposefulness in life coming from God's providential oversight. Every aspect of life has its "time." H. H. Robinson writes, "God is intimately connected with time. . . . His relation to men itself requires the time-order for the fulfillment of his purposes."[2] This approach to time is adopted by the Teacher and made the basis of his optimism. The fourteen couplets covered in 3:2–8 cover the whole range of human activity. Therefore, the Teacher sees God in control of all of life.[3]

Koheleth covers "everything." The following seven verses particularize the opening verse. Two words for time appear in 3:1: "season" and "time." Probably no distinction needs to be drawn of the words. They serve as synonyms. What follows is a list of activities that describes what happens "under heaven."[4]

The systematic passing of time appears in 3:2–8. The poem contains fourteen pairs of contrasting opposites. The use of opposites represents a common figure of speech in Hebrew poetry (merism) to denote completeness. There is a time for this and a time for that—twenty-eight times. The poem begins with a time that life begins for a human being and a time that life ends for human beings. "A time to be born, and a time to die" (3:2a). No person decides when to be born or when to die, unless in the exceptional case of suicide. The time to be born and the time to dies exist beyond human control.

The poem matches the first pair with a second pair: "A time to plant, and a time to pluck up what is planted" (3:2b). Humans do not control the time to plant flowers or fruit trees. It has to be done at the appropriate time in the season. We plant our flowers in the spring, and in the fall we pull them up. Humans can ignore the appropriate time to plant, but it would be a foolish act.

The poem continues with two additional pairs of contrasting opposites: "a time to kill, and a time to heal" (3:3a). The actions represent occasions to end a life and efforts to preserve a life. The poet describes what happens "under heaven." He is not making a moral pronouncement about killing and healing. The killing could refer to war or to the natural ending of a life, and the healing could refer to the attempts to keep the life going. The Teacher pairs "a time to break down, and a time to build up" (3:3b) with "a time to kill and a time to heal." More than likely the Teacher refers to warfare. Attacking armies destroy buildings, but when hostilities cease, the buildings are built again.

Koheleth moves to the realm of emotions in the systematic passing of time. "A time to weep, and a time to laugh; a time to mourn, and a time to dance" (3:4). This verse presents two closely related pairs of contrasting emotions.[5] The Teacher mentions two negative emotions which inevitably come with the systematic passing of time: weeping and mourning. The first part of verse 4 contrasts weeping with laughter. The second part of the verse contrasts mourning and dancing. Michael Eaton thinks the first pair of weeping and laughing represents private emotions, and mourning and dancing pair represents public displays of emotion.[6] Life experiences cause humans to react with different emotions.

The next pair of opposites is hard to categorize. "A time to throw away stones, and a time to gather stones together" (3:5a). The next line does not seem to be related to the first statement in verse 5. "A time to embrace, and a time to refrain from embracing" (3:55b). R. N. Whybray sees the first contrast as "the need to clear away stones from a field in order to make it suitable for agricultural use."[7] The second contrast reflects a great difference with the previous contrast: "A time to embrace, and a time to refrain from embracing" (3:5b). The reference to embracing is often taken to be a romantic embrace. However, it is probably best, as in verse 5a, to take it in a more general sense. The embrace was a common way of greeting friends, as is the handshake today. Either physical absence or anger would prevent a person from embracing. It could be used to apply to types of greetings, good-byes, or welcomes.[8]

The next pair of contrasting opposites refer to possessions. "A time to seek, and a time to lose; a time to keep, and a time to throw away" (3:6). There are times we need to look for something, and there are times we need to give up the search. Then there are times we need to keep possessions and times we need to throw something away.

Many scholars think the next pairing in verse 7 refers to mourning and the termination of mourning. "A time to tear, and a time to sew; a time to keep silent, and a time to speak" (3:7). Tearing could refer to the practice of expressing sorrow such as the rending of one's clothes. Often when people mourned the death of a loved one, they would express sorrow by tearing their clothes. When the time of mourning had passed, they would then mend their clothes. The next line, "a time to keep silence, and a time to speak," seems to go with the first line of verse 7. People expressed their sorrow over losing a loved one by keeping silent. The friends of Job sat with him seven days, and no one spoke a word to Job. The time of speaking may be connected with the proper time to speak.

The final couplet in the poem has pairs of contrasting statements: "a time to love, and a time to hate; a time for war, and a time for peace" (3:8). Two nouns "love" and "hate" are exemplified by "war" and "peace." Together they create a chiasm. The nouns refer to strong emotions of attraction and repulsion. These actions on a public level manifest themselves as states of "peace" and "war." Koheleth does not promote these emotional states or actions, but he simply describes them as a part of the systematic passing of time.

What seems to be the Teacher's purpose in this poem? Evidently his mission is to discern the right and wrong times for conduct and speech. To master life is a part of knowing when to do something and when to do other things. Koheleth leaves it to the reader to discern the situation and decide how to act. Such concern for action appropriate to its time underlies Koheleth's poetical catalogue.[9] Koheleth moves away from the systematic passing of time to reflecting on who controls time.

The Sovereign Control of Time

3:9-11

The first eight verses have asserted a systematic passing of time but with little interpretation or comment. The Teacher has not mentioned God, who began time and controls it. Koheleth finishes the poem about time (3:1-8) and then provides a prose reflection in verses 9-11. In 3:1-8 humanity is the grammatical subject of the various infinitives—people plant and pluck up, mourn and dance. But the human factor does not determine such events. The Teacher clearly thinks God alone is the one who determines the times. The Teacher implies that God is the primary actor on the earthly scene. The systematic passing of time appears to be held firmly by God. In 3:1-8 the Teacher has not said anything about the how and why of the times. He has merely illustrated that there is a systematic time for everything. Beginning in 3:9, the Teacher begins to discern the One who is sovereign over time.

Having implied that God is sovereign over time, the Teacher returned to the subject of work and asked a question he had asked previously in 1:3. "What gain have the workers from their toil?" (3:9). In the continuous quest to find meaning in life, the Teacher always wanted to know what kind of profit he would get for his investment of time and effort. Knowing how hard people toil, he said, " I have seen the business that God has given to everyone to be busy with" (3:10). On first reading one might get the idea that the "business" God gives to human beings merely keeps them busy and that is all.

Up this point the Teacher has merely reported that various activities take place in the passing of time. With a striking surprise in verse 10 Koheleth describes the One who sets the times. The teacher sees God as the One who "has made everything suitable for its times" (3:11a). The "everything" refers back to 3:1, "For everything there is a season, and a time for every matter under heaven." The Teacher continues, "Moreover he has put a sense of past and future into their minds, yet they cannot find out what God has done from the beginning to the end" (3:11b). The Teacher moves from an "under the sun" mentality to the working of God in the created order. The pronoun "he" of verse 11 refers back to God in verse 10. The Teacher's view of the earthly realm of existence is that God's disposal of events in their time is "suitable." The verb "made" means God has caused it to happen. This verb affirms that God caused the universe and all its workings to come into being. "Everything" refers to the comprehensiveness of creation.

"Suitable" can mean "beautiful" or "appropriate." The mention of God's making everything beautiful, appropriate, or suitable could refer back to Genesis 1 where God pronounced each step of his creation as "good" (Gen. 1:4, 10, 12, 18, 21, 31). "Suitable" claims God's unsurpassable sovereignty in and over creation. The Teacher concludes that the "time" of earthly events is from the grounds of despair, but the "time" of earthly events can be a source of delight.

The sovereign control of God on creation continues with an insight about what God does for human beings. "He has put a sense of past and future into their minds, yet they cannot find out what God has done from the beginning to the end" (3:11b). God has put something in human beings that allows them to sense the eternal. Human beings are endowed with the ability to step back from immediate situations and particular events that call for their attention to catch a glimpse of the totality of existence, including their own. Such is the mark of self-consciousness. Though self-consciousness exists, omniscience does not. Humans remain ignorant of any purposeful providence that underlies the totality "from the beginning to the end." The expression "put a sense past and future into their mind" seems to distinguish human beings from the animal world. Humans can study the past and contemplate the future, and animals cannot. Humans have a concern with meaning both in its past and future aspects. No human being can escape this unique trait. Human beings have a deep-seated desire to appreciate the character, composition, and meaning of the world. They desire to discern purpose and destiny. They long for a transcendence of their immediate situation.

The Teacher emphasizes the unique distinction of human beings, but he also stressed that human beings are finite. "Yet they cannot find out what God has done from the beginning to the end." Human beings must accept the fact that they are the created not the Creator. Humans cannot see beyond time into eternity to see as God sees. We cannot comprehend the entire picture. Derek Kidner writes, "We are like the desperately nearsighted, inching their way along some great tapestry or fresco in the attempt to take it in. We see enough to recognize something of its quality, but the grand design escapes us, for we can never stand back far enough to view it as the Creator does, whole and entire, from the beginning to the end."[10]

The Satisfaction of Life within Time

3:12–15

Given the human limitations, people must accept themselves and find their satisfaction. The Teacher puts forth his own knowledge of what is good for human beings and the implication of God's work. He says, "I know" on two occasions (3:12, 14). Life does not have to be all despair. According to Koheleth life can have some satisfaction. He offers suggestions for satisfaction while we live our lives on earth.

Satisfaction comes by enjoying what God gives us. "I know that there is nothing better for them than to be happy and enjoy themselves as long as they live; moreover, it is God's gift that all should eat and drink and take pleasure in their toil" (3:12–13). Human beings need to be busy with the things God has given them. In 3:10 the Teacher spoke of "the business that God has given to the children of man." Now he tells how to go about the business—joyfully, energetically, and with gratitude.

In the earthly realm the Teacher specifies food and drink as expressions of the satisfied life. Toil is also described in terms of satisfaction. Human beings need to accept the simple things of life and enjoy the present to the best of their ability. When Koheleth says there is "nothing better" than enjoying God's gifts, he is not settling for a second-rate existence. He is telling us that there is satisfaction, meaning, and enjoyment in the regular things of everyday life.

Satisfaction also comes by trusting God's sovereignty. "I know that whatever God does endures forever; nothing can be added to it, nor anything taken from it; God has done this, so that all should stand in awe before him" (3:14). Earthly existence is characterized by transitoriness, unreliability, and futility. Security can only be found elsewhere, namely in God's control of human existence.

The Teacher highlights several traits of God's actions. First, God's actions are permanent. "I know that whatever God does endures forever" (3:14a). Satisfaction comes to human beings out of accepting God's sovereignty over time and eternity.

Second, God's actions are effective and complete. "Nothing can be added to it, nor anything take from it" (3:14b). What God wants to do will invariably be done, and no human being can alter the course of God's will by human efforts.

Third, God's actions are secure. No outside force can

threaten to destroy God's work. These actions of God lead human beings to respond in reverence to him. "So that all should stand in awe before him" (3:14c). It is not a terror in the face of a monstrous unknown but an awesome reverence and regard for a gracious God. This is why God has set the times. God's times make human beings aware of their finiteness. God's times make humans aware of their helplessness and their total dependence on God. He is the Sovereign One who controls everything. Trusting God's absolute sovereignty gives humans a great sense of satisfaction.

The Teacher repeats one more time the point that God controls the times. "That which is already has been; that which is to be, already is; and God seeks out what has gone by" (3:15). Whatever happens in the present has happened in the past. It is the same story over and over again. The Teacher puts everything under the sovereignty of God. He helps us make progress in understanding the universe. The things that happen should not cause us to despair but to hope in God, who is sovereign over everything that happens.

The last part of verse 15 is a hopeful trust, "God seeks out what has gone by." James L. Crenshaw suggests that "God ensures that events which have just transpired do not vanish into thin air. God brings them back once more, so that the past circles into the present." [11] We tend to think the past represent days gone forever. Koheleth tells us that God is seeking to recover the past. By God's grace he seeks to rescue and restore what seems to be lost forever.

Koheleth observes an ordered universe. He begins to think a Designer created the universe and sustains it. Human beings have a place in the Designer's creation, but their role is not to redesign the universe. They are to acknowledge the Designer and enjoy the earthly existence the Designer has given them.

Chapter 5

A Look at Human Relationships

3:16–4:16

Life involves a lot of human relationships. The presence of people in our lives creates an interesting dynamic. Like it or not, people have to relate to people. The actions of human relationships are impossible to ignore—trusting one another, listening to one another, doing business with one another, talking with one another, enjoying one another, arguing with one another, avoiding one another, and numerous other "one anothers." No one can live alone. Even the most introverted person craves human contact. People blossom from childhood to adulthood because of the love, encouragement, support, and care from many human beings. But the reverse is also true. Many people suffer from lack of love and care, abuse, injustice, and other negative human reactions.

Once a psychologist friend said to me, "Harold, there is no greater joy in life than a relationship. And there is no greater sorrow in life than a relationship." Think of those qualities we receive from other human beings that give us joy: unconditional love, compassionate understanding, trust with our most confident secrets, forgiveness for our many mistakes, and the intimacy of being known and by knowing one another. Think now of the great sorrow brought by relationships: people making us feel guilty or unworthy, unwarranted prejudices of who we are or where we live, uncontrolled lust leading to sexual abuse, out-of-control anger from another person which threatens our well-being, and numerous other negative attitudes and actions. Everyone has been hurt by another person, and it brings great sorrow.

Koheleth has been looking at life from many angles. He does not neglect the sight of human relationships. Throughout his book of Ecclesiastes, he views good relationships of mutual caring, but he also sees relationships of malicious treatment of others. He sees a world filled with cutthroat competition, wickedness, oppressions, unfairness, and envy. In Ecclesiastes 3:16 Koheleth reports about another sight he got from life. His next observation of life is introduced by the transitional phrase "Moreover, I saw" (3:16a). The experience of the Teacher is captured again by the verb "to see." The Teacher reports what he saw in the section 3:16–4:16. In this section the theme focuses on unhealthy relationships. Koheleth mentions four prominent actions that hurt human relationships: injustice, oppression, envy, and isolation.

Injustice

3:16-22

Kohelth begins by reporting that he sees injustices among human beings where he expected justice, namely in the law courts. "Moreover I saw under the sun that in the place of righteousness, wickedness was there as well" (3:16). In the Western world a court of law can often be identified by the sculpture of a woman holding a set of scales. The woman is Lady Justitia. She weighs carefully what is just and what is unjust, what is right and what is wrong.[1] Koheleth sees guilt and innocence confused in the law court. The innocent are judged guilty and the guilty judged innocent. Koheleth questions whether a person can expect to receive what he or she really deserves.

At the law courts where judicial procedures are in progress and where righteousness could be expected, wickedness was found instead. In place of the law courts being places of justice, they were places of injustice. As we have seen before in Ecclesiastes, the phrase "under the sun" describes the futility and meaninglessness of life lived purely for self without regard for God and his ways. What Koheleth sees "under the sun" is unfortunate injustice of human beings to other human beings.

The Teacher proceeds to reflect on what he saw in the law courts: "I said in my heart" (3:17a). He reasons that if there is a season for everything, "a time for every matter under heaven," then there must be a time for justice. Rather than getting angry and sad about the injustices, Koheleth seems to trust God to make things right. "I said in my heart, God will judge the righteous and the wicked, for he has appointed a time for every matter, and for every work" (3:17). The Teacher thinks that ultimately the innocent and the guilty will get what they deserve from the hand of God. The Teacher does not seem to be thinking about God's final judgment at the end of time. He is simply saying, "God will judge in his own time."[2] No human being knows the time God will judge.

The Teacher has not settled the issue of injustice in place of justice in the law courts. The phrase "I said in my heart" (3:18a) could indicate an inner dialogue or struggle between two opposing ideas within the mind of Koheleth. If there is no justice in the present, does an afterlife settle the issue of justice? "I said in my heart with regard to human beings that God is testing them to show that they are but animals. For the fate of humans and the fate of animals is the same; as one dies, so does the other. They all have the same breath, and humans have no advantage over the animals; for all is vanity. All go to one place; all are from the dust, and all turn to dust again. Who knows whether the human spirit goes upward and the spirit of animals goes downward to the earth?" (3:18-21). He gives a similarity between animals and humans. Both have the same breath, and both die. When the human and the animal die, the breath goes away. Humans have no advantage over animals with respect to death. Both animals and humans return to dust.

Koheleth wonders if there is something special about humans. He raises a question. "Who knows whether the human spirit goes upward and the spirit of animals goes downward to the earth?" (3:21). On many occasions Jewish teachers made positive statements with the use of rhetorical questions. Koheleth seems to indicate that at death the spirit of a human goes upward to the heavens rather than downward to Sheol. The Teacher thinks humans differ from animals. The spirit of the human goes "upward." Though Koheleth seems to conceive of life after death for humans, he does not elucidate its quality. He merely indicates that God takes human life in a different manner from that of the animal.

The inner struggle seemed too much for Koheleth; therefore he came back to think of the present earthly existence. If justice cannot be found in the present and if justice is uncertain for the future, human beings need to take advantage of enjoyment afforded to them in the present. "So I saw there is nothing better than all should enjoy their work, for that is their lot; who can bring them to see what will be after them?" (3:22). Humans have to work to live. So they might as well enjoy their work with its results. Again, Koheleth asks a question, "Who can bring them to see what will be after them?" The expected answer is: no one can. From observations of life on earth, no one knows better whether the human spirit goes upward after death, and no one knows what will be after death. Therefore, humans might as well make the best of their brief existence on earth.

Oppression

4:1-3

The Teacher continues to look at human relationships. In this scene he sees another unhealthy interpersonal relationship. He has observed injustices, and now he observes oppression. He moves to the subject of oppression with the phrase, "Again I saw" (4:1a). He is an eyewitness of harsh treatment of human beings to other human beings. He mentions oppression three times in 4:1: "oppressions," "oppressed," and "oppressors." Iain Provan writes, "Oppression involves cheating one's neighbor of something . . . defrauding him, and robbing him. . . . It is the abuse of power, financial and otherwise, perpetrated on those who are not so powerful and are indeed vulnerable—the poor, widows, orphans, and strangers."[3]

The sight of the oppressed distressed the Teacher. "Again I saw all the oppressions that are practiced under the sun. Look, the tears of the oppressed—with no one to comfort them! On the side of the oppressors there was power—with no one to comfort them" (4:1). There is no one to comfort the oppressed by protecting them from the abuse of their oppressors. The oppressed weep over their dilemma. No one comforts abused slaves, battered women, exploited children, and cheated workers. The Teacher is distressed that oppression should have power at all. The repetition of "with no one to comfort them" heightens the sense of human helplessness. Earthly comforters fail to provide help for the hurting. The Teacher and others seem helpless to stop the oppressors. Earthly resources give no relief.

The wickedness of no one's coming forward to help oppressed people greatly distressed the Teacher. He became so disgusted that he concluded the dead are more fortunate than the living. "And I thought the dead, who have already died, more fortunate than the living, who are still alive" (4:2). Seeing the oppressed brings great distress to the living eyewitnesses. The dead no longer have to witness the awful wicked oppressions in society. Koheleth concludes that it is better off to be dead than to live in such a world filled with the sight of human oppression.

Koheleth continues with another thought. "But better than both is the one who has never been, and has not see the evil deeds that are done under the sun" (4:3). The unborn are more fortunate that those alive and even those who have died. The unborn have never been an eyewitness to the evil oppressions committed "under the sun."

Koheleth's sentiment resembles both Job and Jeremiah.

"Let the day perish in which I was born, and the night that said, 'A man-child is conceived.' Let that day be darkness! May the God above not seek it, or light shine on it. Let gloom and deep darkness claim it. Let clouds settle upon it; let the blackness of the day terrify it" (Job 3:3–5). "Why did I come from the womb to see toil and sorrow, and spend my days in shame" (Jer. 20:18).

Envy

4:4–6

The Teacher has seen two forms of wickedness: injustices in the court of law and people being mistreated by others and no one stopping to help them. Now the Teacher moves to another expression of wickedness in human behavior: "Then I saw" (4:4a). This again is a typical pattern in how the Teacher moves from one idea to another idea. This time the Teacher observes unbelievable envy. "Then I saw that all toil and all skill in work come from one person's envy of another. This also is vanity and a chasing after wind" (4:4). Koheleth sees toil and success in work. He sees that both of these results come from envy. As people look at the accomplishments of other people, they work harder in order to get ahead and to stay ahead of them.

The application of one's talents and gifts would seem to capture the essence of meaningful work. But the Teacher probes deeper and finds that at its root lies an ulterior motive for work, namely envy. Envy inspires ruthless competition and distorts the nobler sense of vocation with an exercise in rivalry into a quest for dominance, leading many times to violence.[4]

Koheleth exposes the danger of any work that becomes a means of gaining supremacy over another person. The envy of another contradicts the great command in Leviticus to "love your neighbor as yourself " (Lev. 19:18b). Koheleth sees only a selfish motive, getting ahead of one's neighbor, behind work. This motive can never be satisfied, so it leads to ceaseless work and despair. It is a "chasing after wind."

Why do people overwork and spend their lives that way? People may say they are simply making a living, supporting their family, enjoying their work, or contributing to society. The Teacher disagrees. He claims that the basic motivation for our striving is rivalry. People want the top spot. They want to be better than the next person. They crave to be recognized as the best. Charles Swindoll calls Ecclesiastes 4:1-8 "The Lonely Whine of the Top Dog."[5] Koheleth says the ruthless competition with one another to gain greater stuff is vanity. It is futile. It leaves us empty. It is a chasing after the wind.

The Teacher sketches three options of how people can cope with a competitive world. Since people work with their hands, he gives three options with three positions of the hands. First, the Teacher mentions the folded hands. "Fools fold their hands and consume their own flesh" (4:5). Of course the Teacher is being sarcastic and using hyperbole when he talks about them eating their own flesh. The folded hands picture people who do not want to work. The Teacher calls these people "fools." The Teacher implies that these people kill themselves by starvation. The picture is one who has dropped from the rat race with its hectic scramble for status to the dropout of total indifference.

The second option is to cup open the hands to acquire as much as possible. Two hands can hold much more than one open hand. "Better is a handful with quiet than two handfuls with toil, and a chasing after wind" (4:6). In this verse the Teacher used a "better than" proverb. The way of wisdom will attempt much (a handful) but not too much (two handfuls). People often think bigger is better and more is better. There is a downside to selecting two handfuls. It involves "toil and chasing after wind." In order to get the two handfuls, people have to resort to excessive toil—work, work, work. Unremitting work is a hallmark of oppression. William P. Brown writes, "Without the benefit of rest, even self-employment is self-enslavement."[6] In the end the work-work-work turns out to be two handfuls of wind, meaninglessness.

The third option is one handful. "Better is a handful with quiet" (4:6a). A handful refers to a small amount (cf. 1

Kings 17:12). This small amount leads to being "quiet." Richard Foster in his book *The Freedom of Simplicity* teaches that the simple life leads to a more tranquil life.[7] The simple life is not cumbered with a lot of stuff. The point of Koheleth's passage is to be content with one handful and enjoy our work with quietness. The handful with quiet represents the middle way between the clamorous grasping of toil and skill and the escapism of folded hands of doing nothing.

Isolation

4:7-16

The theme of excessive work spills over into the next thought block in 4:7-16. The Teacher addressed a human relationship problem of cutthroat competition born out of selfish envy. Now he moves to the problem of isolation or individualism. Notice how Koheleth moves smoothly to another insight: "Again, I saw" (4:7a). "Again, I saw vanity under the sun: the case of solitary individuals, without sons or brothers; yet there is no end to all their toil, and their eyes are never satisfied with riches. 'For whom am I toiling,' they ask, 'and depriving myself of pleasure?' This also is vanity and an unhappy business" (4:7-8). Koheleth gives the sad picture of a person who had no human relationships. The world "solitary" indicates that the person had no friend, no wife, or business partner. Also, he did not have "sons or brothers," the two closest relationships who might benefit from his inheritance. The Teacher pictures the person spending his time working hard to acquire wealth and never deriving any pleasure from the wealth that is the result of his efforts.

The Teacher asks an abrupt question, "For whom am I toiling?" The answer is self-reflexive: "I am toiling for myself." The loneliness in Koheleth's eyes gives evidence of having sacrificed all form of relationships upon the altar of self-centeredness. Koheleth appropriately concludes the illustration of people working and not having relationships with the words "vanity and an unhappy business." Remember, "There is no greater joy in life than a relationship." Now the tones seem to say, "There is no greater emptiness in life than the absence of a relationship."

In contrast to the loner (one) are companions or friends (two). Compare the solitary persons life with that of a person who has a "second," a companion. "Two are better than one, because they have a good reward for their toil" (4:9). The Teacher has indicated in 4:6 more is not better with reference to possessions. But, when it comes to relationships, more is better.

Koheleth gives three illustrations to show two are better than one. First, he pictures a person needing help on the road. "For if they fall, one will lift up the other; but woe to the one who is alone and falls and does not have another to help" (4:10). Koheleth knows about traveling in the Middle East. It can be dangerous, especially on dark nights. People can easily stumble and plunge down an embankment. A companion is able to rescue a fellow traveler. Temper Longman III writes that "it may also teach that companionship is important when one encounters any difficulty in life."[8]

Koheleth's second illustration of the benefit of companionship is about people sleeping together to keep each other warm. "Again, if two lie together, they keep warm; but how can one keep warn alone?" (4:11). Michael Eaton thinks this illustration could refer to husband and wife or to travelers in Israel's cold nights sleeping together for warmth.[9]

The third illustration comes also from traveling in the Middle East. Many robbers roamed the land. "And though one might prevail against another, two will withstand one" (4:12a). The lonely traveler may be overpowered by a robber. Safety is found in companionship.

The three illustrations close with a proverb: "A threefold cord is not quickly broken" (4:12b). A threefold cord is a rope with three strands twisted together. A single cord can be easily broken. Like the previous illustrations, one alone might not survive a fall, keep warm on a cold night, or withstand a robber alone. From the repetition of two, two, two, Koheleth moves to three in the proverb about the rope. Michael Eaton thinks "that companionship may operate within large numbers."[10] Strength may be gained by growing interdependence. The Teacher's message is that relationship of togetherness is better than solidarity.

The Teacher closes with a story that develops the idea of isolation versus companionship. "Better is a poor but wise youth than an old but foolish king, who will no longer take advice. One can indeed come out of prison to reign, even though poor born in the kingdom. I saw all the living who, moving about under the sun, follow that youth who replaced the king; there was no end to all those people whom he led. Yet those who come later will not rejoice in him. Surely this also is vanity and a chasing after wind" (4:13-16). Koheleth tells of an old and foolish king. He would not take advice. He had isolated himself. This king like the rich man in 4:8 became a solitary individual. He had no relationship with advisors.

Koheleth mentions one who came out of prison to reign. This could have been a reference to Joseph who came out of prison in Egypt to rule in the nation. Whoever this young man was, he did not choose to live the solitary life like the foolish king. He was one with all the people he led. The wise youth made a wise king. A third character appears in the illustration. "Yet those who come later will not rejoice in him" (4:16b). People will no longer follow the young king when he becomes old. The second young man is soon forgotten with the passing of time. Again think of Joseph. He had had such great wisdom. He was a great ruler. But "a new king arose over Egypt, who did not know Joseph" (Exod. 1:8).

The illustration concludes with a familiar statement. "Surely this also is vanity and a chasing after wind" (4:16b). Even a life that attains the pinnacle of human success, even a life adorned by millions, even a life blessed with wisdom is useless in the end. The pursuits are called "chasing after wind." Life is empty. The life and deeds of a popular king are soon forgotten.

Koheleth looked at a world filled with human relationships. Thankfully he sees the happiness of healthy relationships. He agrees that nothing brings greater joy than a relationship. But unfortunately his look at life continues to be absolutely honest, and he reports dysfunctional relationships. He sees injustices in the law courts, pain and sorrow in the lives of innocent people who have been oppressed by others. He sees people trying to get ahead of one another in a dog-eat-dog world. He sees a culture marked by rugged individualism caused by a selfish disposition. He would also agree that a relationship brings the greatest sorrow in life.

Chapter 6

The Sight of Attenders at the House of God

5:1-7

The message of Ecclesiastes has become clear even to the casual reader. All is vanity or meaningless under the sun, and in all of our work we find no real gain or profit. The Teacher has pounded the theme of vanity in chapters 1-4. Ecclesiastes 5:1-7 comes as quite a shock. The Teacher moves for a while from his theme of vanity and meaninglessness to provide readers with some words of advice. The Teacher reports observations he has made. In chapters 1-4 he tells of insight he got from the world. Now in chapter 5 he reports on the observation he had of people going to the house of God. The world has left him rather skeptical and sad, and maybe he looks toward the house of God for hope. The tone of Koheleth's discourse shifts in 5:1 from objective observation to admonition. The Teacher shifts to imperatives and injunctions rather than assuming his audience will understand the implications of his observations.[1]

The Teacher begins his words of advice by making several

admonitions to the attendees at the house of God. Koheleth makes an observation of people going and coming to the house of God or the place of worship. Tucked into his words on worship, the Teacher manages to highlight unhealthy practices that make worship itself meaningless, vain, absurd, and fruitless. The Teacher offers some sound advice about how to worship, but that advice exists against a backdrop of those who manage to be "fools" even in their attempt to worship God. The Teacher treats worship in terms of sacrifice (5:1), prayers (5:2-3), and vows (5:4-7). In participating in sacrifice, prayers, and vows, one can do any one or all of them as a fool. The foolish action runs throughout the section of 5:1-7. It is a sad fact of life that human beings can take something like worship and pervert it.[2]

In previous sections of Ecclesiastes, the Teacher has offered reports on his observations. He mainly leaves the reader's opinion open to the choice of the audience. But in Ecclesiastes 5 Koheleth becomes more of an adviser than an observer. He reports what he sees, but he gives straightforward advice about worship. In Ecclesiastes 5:1-7 we come to a section where Koheleth sounds less like an agnostic, which he might have sounded like in Ecclesiastes chapters 1-4. The Teacher demonstrates in 5:1-7 that he has a deep interest in God and that he is extremely perceptive about the true manner of worship. The section gives us a picture that the Teacher is closer to genuine Old Testament piety than we have imagined in the earlier chapters of Ecclesiastes.

Ecclesiastes 5:1-7 is unique in Ecclesiastes because it focuses on worship at the house of God. This section helps counter the trend of turning worship into religious entertainment or meaningless ritual. This text has admonitions or imperatives to help people worship God correctly. These imperatives give the tone of advice rather than mere insights. Koheleth realizes that people stand in need of an altogether greater companionship or relationship with God. Earlier the Teacher has told of a God who gives joy and pleasure. Can a person relate to this God? This question is answered in terms of the house of God, obedience, sacrifice, prayer, and vows. If God is in heaven and he is the ruler and judge, he cannot be approached casually. Koheleth assumes that God may be approached, addressed in conversation, and will receive human vows. The Teacher gives thought blocks from the section on how worship should happen.

Approach God Reverently

5:1a

Evidently Koheleth watched people closely as they attended the house of God. Oddly enough the Teacher began his treatment of worship before the people ever got to the house of God. He gives his first command about worship in 5:1: "Guard your steps when you go to the house of God." Fruitful and acceptable worship begins before it formally begins. It begins before attenders ever get to the house of God. Without a doubt worship could be enriched by preparing days before going into the presence of God.

The Teacher tells his readers to exercise caution when they go to the house of God for worship. You are not just going to be with a few friends. You are not going to be entertained by the musicians. You are not going merely to be seen as an attender at the house of God. You are not going to give allegiance to a minister. You are going to "the house of God." You are going to the place where the almighty Creator and Redeemer comes to meet with you. "Guard your steps!"

What is the likelihood that good will come out of going to the house of God with people who think and talk about everything but worship when they come? Alexander MacLaren writes, "Hearts that have no dew of previous preparation to make them receptive are not likely to drink in much of the showers of blessing which may be falling around them."[3] The expression "guard your steps" refers to demeanor and preparedness as one comes to worship. It would involve getting ready to listen to God; it would mean getting ready to accept what God has to say; it would mean getting our mind and heart prepared for a meeting with God.

Worship is about entering the presence of God. Be careful.

If we are going into the presence of One who is so great, so powerful, so holy, so awesome, so majestic, we are about to put ourselves in a serious situation. We dare not go into the house of God casually, flippantly, routinely, or thoughtlessly. The term "house of God" was common in the literature of the second-temple era. The Teacher recognizes the role worship plays in establishing and maintaining a meaningful existence.

Koheleth focused on God in 5:1–7. He mentions God six times in these verses. God is the prominent One in worship. He is the audience for the attendants at worship. Remember Moses' meeting with God at the burning bush. God said to him, "Remove the sandals from your feet, for the place on which you are standing is holy ground" (Exod. 3:5). "Guard your steps," says the Teacher. Approach God reverently. Worship experiences are great blessings when the heart and mind have been in a state of preparation before the formal time of worship. Maybe it was no accident that the Jewish Sabbath began at sunset on Friday evening. It gave worshipers time to "guard their steps" before they came the next day on Saturday to the temple, synagogue, or any other place of worship.

Listen to God Carefully

5:1b-3

After admonishing worshippers to approach God reverently, Koheleth commands them to listen to God carefully. "Better than the sacrifice offered by fools; for they do not know how to keep from doing evil. Never be rash with your mouth, nor let your heart be quick to utter a word before God, for God is in heaven, and you upon earth; therefore let your words be few. For dreams come with many cares, and a fool's voice with many words" (5:1b-3). In the temple, while sacrifices were offered to God, "silence reigned, fostering a sense of divine presence and human receptivity."[4]

After the sacrifices had been offered, the priest would read from the Hebrew Scriptures and explain what he read. He would then offer prayers, and the people would respond with songs. And finally the priest would place God's blessing on the people.

According to the Teacher listening to God's Word was better than the sacrifices offered by fools. The term "fools" refers to those who bring unacceptable sacrifices to God. People are fools when they bring to God what they cannot use themselves—blind, lame, or sick animals. These fools think their sacrifices will cancel out their sins without the need for repentance.[5] These people are so foolish that they are not even aware that their sacrifices are evil, an offense to God.

In contrast to the busy fools, Koheleth advises worshippers to listen. "To draw near to listen is better than the sacrifice offered by fools; for they do not know how to keep from doing evil" (5:1b). When silence occurs in worship, a sense of divine presence happens, and a human receptivity becomes possible. Many times God said to Israel, "Hear, O Israel." Israel was commanded to listen to God's instructions. Jesus emphasized the importance of listening with his frequent words, "He who has ears, let him hear." James strongly commanded listening, "Let everyone be quick to listen, slow to speak, slow to anger" (James 1:19).

Koheleth warns the attendants at the house of God not to badger God with superfluous talk. The fool may offer his sacrifice with mechanical apathy, but the wise person will be receptive toward the teaching of God from the priests. Listen to the teacher's caution: "Never be rash with your mouth, nor let your heart be quick to utter a word before God, for God is in heaven, and you upon the earth; therefore let your words be few" (5:2). Just as one exercises the utmost care when speaking to a person with an exalted position in society, so one has to be even more careful in the presence of an exalted God. The Teacher describes the distance of a holy God from finite human beings. God is in heaven, and we are on earth. God is far above us, far superior to us. So we should certainly watch our speech when we meet with almighty God in his house. Rudolph Otto thinks liturgical silence is a way of encountering the holy. He thinks silence is "no mere momentary pause, but an absolute cessation of sound long enough to 'hear the silence' itself."[6] The ever-present practice of verbosity takes away the time for the awesome power of the listening ear. So, out of reverence for almighty God, Koheleth admonishes us to give priority to listening rather than talking with him.

The Teacher supports the idea of few words with a proverb. "For dreams come with many cares, and a fool's voice with many words" (5:3). The proverb assumes that many cares will lead to dreams. Alexander MacLaren made a good explanation of Ecclesiastes 5:3: "What is condemned is words which travel faster than thoughts and feelings, or which proceed from hearts that have not been brought into patient submission, or form such a lack of reverent realization of God's majesty."[7] Words lead to many dreams. Foolishness leads to many words. Maybe hard work tears a person down so that one starts to lose touch with reality. The foolish think their many words have an apparent effect on God.

Make Commitments to God Seriously

5:4-6

Koheleth now moves to another piece of advice for worship attenders. This admonition involves care in making vows to God. Like sacrifice and listening, a vow is a sacred tribute to God. When taking a vow, worshippers commit themselves to undertake some kind of action. Foolish worship involves those who make a vow to God and then have no hurry or desire to pay what they have promised to God. Attenders have no difficulty remembering God is in heaven while they are on a troubled earth. They have no problem going to God when they have a problem they want him to solve. But after making a promise to God, they forget about who God is.

Koheleth begins his discussion on vows with the advice not to delay the action promised to God. "When you make a vow to God, do not delay fulfilling it; for he has no pleasure in fools. Fulfill what you vow" (5:4). Usually a vow involves a conditional promise made to God. If God will do something for the worshipper, then the worshipper will do something for God. Unfortunately, worshippers on many occasions fail to fulfill their vows to God. A wise worshipper does not delay in fulfilling a vow to God.

God does not take vows made to him lightly. "He has no pleasure in fools." Again the word "fool" appears. In this case it refers to a person who does not act wisely in that a vow is made and then the promise is not fulfilled by that person. Worshippers need to take seriously the vows they make to God. "It is better that you should not vow than that you should vow and not fulfill it"(5:5). Remember the incident in the church in Jerusalem with Ananias and Sapphira. They vowed to give the church the entire proceeds from the sale of some property. But they kept back a part of the proceeds for themselves, and they were punished with death.

Think for a moment about the vows people make in God's house today. In many cases two people get married in a place of worship, and they promise to live together as husband and wife until death parts them. At children's dedications, parents promise to live an exemplary life before their children and instruct them in the way of the Lord. At baptism people promise to live a life committed to Christ. When church leaders are ordained, they promise to fulfill their calling carefully. Even as people sing hymns in a worship service, they make promises to God, "Take my silver and my gold; not a mite would I withhold." People make private promises to God: "If you heal me Lord, I will..." "If you get me this job, I will..." "If you get me out of this trouble, I will..." Making a promise is easier than keeping it. Koheleth says it is better not to make a vow if you do not intend to keep it.

Koheleth thinks that making a vow to God and not keeping

it is a sin. "Do not let your mouth lead you into sin, and do not say before the messengers that it was a mistake; why should God be angry at your words, and destroy the work of your hands?" (5:6). We can sin in many ways with our words. What the Teacher has in mind in verse 6 is the great sin of making a promise to God and then not keeping that promise. The Teacher mentions the word "messenger." This word could have several meanings. It could refer to an angel, a prophet, a priest, or a messenger sent by a priest. Michael A. Eaton thinks the Teacher pictures a priest or his messenger coming to check on vows people made. The worshipper passes off to the messenger with a flippant response, "Oh, that was a mistake." But God sees and hears promises, and a careless approach may bring his judgment upon our words.[8]

Koheleth does not call for the absence of human words in worship. Instead, he wants spoken words to be spoken with a serious commitment. He thinks it would be better not to make a vow than to make a vow and not keep it. The Teacher expresses a grave concern for worshippers to take seriously the commitments they make to God.

Fear God Constantly

5:7

Koheleth moves to his last admonition about worship. This advice urges the worshiper to think of worship as a relationship with God. "With many dreams come vanities and a multitude of words; but fear God" (5:7). Once again the Teacher mentions the association of dreams with many words. Temper Longman III thinks "the point of comparison is fantasy."[9] Dreams are out of touch with reality and so are many words in a cultic setting. The Teacher urges worship attenders to get away from a casual familiarity with God and move toward a serious relationship.

The admonition to "fear God" does not mean a terror in his presence. It means a reverence and an awesome regard for God. In the wisdom tradition the "fear" of God is the holy cause that arises from the realization of being in the presence of the greatness of God: splendor, majesty, power, justice, righteousness, grace, and mercy.

The "fear" of God indicates the transcendence or the enormous distance of God from human beings. But, according to the Old Testament, God does not seem to be so distant that he does not make himself imminent or unavailable to human beings. Deeply implied then in the fear of God is the wonderful possibility of human beings relating to God.

Relating to God involves being responsible to him. How can there be a relationship with God if there is no responsibility to him? Therefore, the "fear" of God means that not only do worshippers relate to him but they also obey him.

The term "fear of God" of Ecclesiastes 5:7 represents the theological center of the book. Those who fear God will guard their steps in going to the house of God. They will prepare. They will be fully aware of who God is in that he is in heaven and humans are on earth. Those who fear God will listen to what he has to say. They will make vows, and then they will fulfill their vows. Those who fear God will have a personal relationship with him, and they will find worship to be meaningful rather then meaningless.

Chapter 7

A Glimpse of People's Mania for Money

5:8-20

Throughout the course of history, human beings seem to have an obsession with the accumulation of wealth. They desperately want to be rich. People invest in stocks and bonds hoping their investments will yield great dividends. Workers search for higher paying jobs so they can have more money. Some go to casinos and gamble in hopes they will win a lot of money. People purchase lottery tickets expecting to become a multimillionaires. Many hope relatives will leave a large inheritance that will make them rich.

When Koheleth wrote Ecclesiastes, he observed the mass mania for money. Israel had become a province in the huge empire ruled by the Ptolemies in Egypt. It was a time of economic development. International trade was booming. Opportunities existed for entrepreneurs to make large fortunes. Money as a means of exchange assumed an importance it never had before. The Teacher observed all of this economic development and this mania for money. The Teacher wants to tell his readers about money and to encourage them to invest in the great values of God's gifts. In Koheleth's reflection on the mania for money, he makes six stimulating insights.

Money Breeds Injustice

5:8-9

Koheleth begins his observation of money with insights of government officials exploiting the poor in order to gain more money. Money has built in it a deep desire to get more even if injustice to others has to be committed. The Teacher talks about the injustices people suffer from the sinful structures of society. "If you see in a province the oppression of the poor and the violation of justice and right, do not be amazed at the matter; for the high official is watched by a higher, and there are yet higher ones over them" (5:8). The Teacher first sees the injustices committed against people who are poor. He describes a system that has so much greed for monetary gain that the welfare of the less fortunate is not considered. In such a system poor people do not have a chance for progress or even justice. They continue to be poor and to become even poorer. Somehow poor people always get the worst end. Koheleth tells his readers not to be surprised with these injustices.

The Teacher sees a governmental hierarchy in which one person oversees another. A key word in 5:8 is the word "watched." It means people in government constantly look out for one another. They protect one another. They have no concern for the poor. Actually, they take material advantage of the poor in every way they can. Their desire to "watch out" for one another comes from the inner disposition of a mania to get more money for themselves.

Koheleth sees that profits are taken from the less fortunate. "But all things considered, there is a advantage for a land: a king for a plowed field" (5:9). The greed for gain goes to the very top. Even the king takes advantage by virtue of his politically powerful position to get the profit of the land. Oftentimes when leaders hold powerful positions, they get a false sense of who they really are, and they think of "right" for them as getting more for themselves. Material possessions have a way of breeding greed and a mania for more. This mania reduces the value of people, and injustices are directed toward the unfortunate.

Money Does Not Bring Satisfaction

5:10–12

The Teacher shifts from governmental greed to greed in general. In Ecclesiastes 5:10–12 there is a chain of proverbs with the proverb in verse 10 stating the idea that money does not satisfy. The next two verses, 11–12, supply additional illustrations of that main idea of verse 10. The Teacher raises the issue of the love of money. "The lover of money will not be satisfied with money; nor the lover of wealth, with gain. This also is vanity" (5:10). Of course wealth or money is not the real problem. The problem is an obsessive attitude with wealth and money. People place wealth and money as the primary pursuit of their lives. They live for money—never mind if it violates justice.[1] No matter how much money people have, they always want more. Those who set money as their highest goal in life will have a never-ending task. They will never reach their goal, and life will be "vanity," meaningless. Money has many good uses, but when it becomes an end in itself, people will end up empty and frustrated.

Human beings make a desperate search for satisfaction. The search involves acquiring something beyond what they have that will satisfy their deep longings. Koheleth has made clear in other places that wisdom, work, entertainment, wine, and women will not bring ultimate satisfaction. The Teacher made explicitly clear that the lover of money will not be ultimately satisfied with any of these. Augustine in the fourth century began his work Confession: "Almighty God, You have made us for yourself, and our hearts are restless till they find their rest in you."[2]

Human beings are "wired" for fellowship with God. Any other arrangement will not bring ultimate satisfaction.

Money Breeds Parasites

5:11

When people get money, they seem to acquire a large number of new "friends." "When goods increase, those who eat them increase, and what gain has their owners but to see them with his eyes?" (5:11). Such individuals may be sponging family members, envious employers, or "newfound friends." Many rich people experience a lot of admirers and hangers-on.

Those who have lots of money seldom have the opportunity to enjoy their earnings. The phrase "those who eat them increase" refers to persons who consume a rich person's wealth. Of course it could be the government with the high tax bracket. Or it could be the irresponsible children of the rich person. Charities also fill the rich man's mailboxes with requests for donations. All the rich person can do is "see them with his eyes." He merely watches as other people consume his goods. Riches have a way of disappearing down a drain of increased responsibilities. The wage earner sees others enjoying his earnings.

Money Causes Restless Nights

5:12

Having made the point that people pursue wealth for satisfaction, the Teacher now moves toward a similar characteristic that the mania for money causes. It causes sleepless nights. "Sweet is the sleep of laborers, whether they eat little or much; but the surfeit of the rich will not let them sleep" (5:12). The "laborers" could refer to the oppressed mentioned in 5:8. Sometimes they have little food to eat. But whether they eat little or much, they sleep well. Koheleth compares the bliss of rest of the laborers with the overindulgence of the rich. The laborers are able to rest, regardless of the amount of food they have. The rich, however, are incessantly preoccupied with the consumption that causes them sleepless nights. Derek Kidner thinks that a lot of exercise machines and health clubs represent efforts "to undo the damage of money and ease."[3]

Koheleth seems to think the mania for the accumulation of wealth could not be good for your health.

Numerous worries come with the pursuit of possessions: Will my children exhaust my financial resources? Will someone take my money from me illegally? Will the stock market crash? Will my business or vocation become obsolete? Will inflation reduce my resources? These questions and numerous others cause the person pursuing money for satisfaction to look at a lot of late-night television, take a lot of sleeping pills, and live constantly on antidepressants. Contentment, as one thinks, is not the abundance of money. Money seems to breed restlessness and destroy contentment.

Money May Be Here Today and Gone Tomorrow

5:13-17

Koheleth now moves to those who have had wealth and lost it. It was with them one day, and it was gone the next day. The Teacher gives the illustration in verses 13–17 of a person toiling and saving his money. The person brought harm to himself though self-deprivation and worry. But the person accumulated vast wealth. Then in one swoop this person lost his wealth with a bad investment. The man has a son, but he cannot support him. Also, he has no inheritance for the son. Eventually the man leaves the world with nothing. It is the story of a man who ruined his life twice. First, he ruined his life in acquiring wealth. His love of wealth was a grievous evil, vanity, and meaningless, a chasing after wind. Second, he ruined his life in losing his wealth. At the end of his life, he could not support his family or leave them an inheritance.

The Teacher talks about the insecurity of money. "There is a grievous ill that I have seen under the sun: riches were kept by their owners to their hurt, and those riches were lost in a bad venture; though they are parents of children, they have nothing in their hands" (5:13-14). The illustration has painful movement: wealth acquired (5:13), wealth lost (5:14a), inability to give inheritance to son (5:14b), inability to take any wealth with you after death (5:15), and then the grim view of life from the one who lost his wealth (5:16).

The Teacher calls a person's loss of wealth "a grievous ill." It is a sickening experience. The situation that caused the person's loss of wealth is not specified. The riches were suddenly and catastrophically lost, whether in a misguided venture or in a sudden reversal of circumstances. One's mind immediately goes to Job whose wealth was devastated though a series of different misfortunes. Overnight Job became poor.

The Teacher paints a graphic picture with the words, "They have nothing in their hands." A lifetime of work, a lifetime of saving and investing, and it is all gone. The expression "they are parents of children" seems to communicate the sadness they have in that they have nothing to leave as an inheritance with their children.

The tragic picture can be summarized with the adage: "You can't take it with you." Human existence involves birth, life on earth, and then death. One comes into the world naked and with nothing to call her own, and she leaves in the same state. Listen to Job: "Naked I came from my mother's womb, and naked shall I return there" (Job1:21). If wealth is not lost from life's vicissitudes, then by death riches gained are inevitably lost. "As they came from their mother's womb, so they shall go again, naked as they came; they shall take nothing for their toil, which they may carry away with their hands. This also is a grievous ill: just as they came, so shall they go; and what gain do they have from toiling for the wind" (5:15–16). Human beings exit life as they entered it. The Teacher asks, "What gain do they have from toiling?" They have no gain. They grab for the wind, but it slips through their fingers. Likewise, wealth slips through your fingers either from a sad misfortune or an ultimate death.

The Teacher gives one of the many reasons not to live for money. "Besides, all their days they eat in darkness, in much vexation and sickness and resentment"(5:17). This is a pathetic picture of greed. Derek Kidner says, "If anything is worse than the addiction money brings, it is the emptiness it leaves."[4] Human beings with eternity in their hearts need better nourishment than possessions. The emptiness wealth leaves is described in four words: darkness, vexation, sickness, and resentment. Darkness symbolizes a person's misery. Sickness points to the mental and physical strain gained in working for wealth. Vexation indicates the cares and frustrations that tore at his mind and heart. Resentment speaks of the time he was enraged over thwarted ambitions and schemes.[5]

Money Represents a Gift of God

5:18-20

The Teacher closes his reflection on money with a striking contrast of the person described in 5:17. In verse 17 readers see a person living for the purpose of gaining wealth. His primary thought was on money. But at the end the Teacher pictures his great distress. Life does not have to end so tragically. Beginning in 5:18 the Teacher deliberately contrasts the fool's life. "This is what I have seen to be good: it is fitting to eat and drink and find enjoyment in all the toil which one toils under the sun the few days of the life God gives us; for this is our lot. Likewise all to whom God gives wealth and possessions and whom he enables to enjoy them, and to accept their lot and find enjoyment in their toil—this is the gift of God. For they will scarcely brood over the days of their lives, because God keeps them occupied with the joy of their hearts" (5:18-20). Beginning in 5:18 the Teacher deliberately contrasts the fool's life reflected in verse 18. He begins the contrast with, "This is what I have seen to be good." Over against a life fraught with resentment (5:13-17), the Teacher offers a way of contentment. Unlike the obsessive quest for gain, the simple pleasure of sustenance and work somehow find their satisfying experience in a limited life.

In light of acquiring wealth being like the chasing of the wind and the absolute certainty of death, Koheleth claims that the best a person can do is to enjoy the life God has given during earth's short existence. The key word in 5:18-20 is "God," and the answer to life held out by the Teacher is openness to God. These two verses are the fifth occurrence of the advice to enjoy God (2:24; 3:12; 3:22; 8:15). The Teacher makes four straightforward statements: First, he says God gives life (5:18). Second, he states that God gives riches (5:19a). Third, God gives the ability to enjoy life's simple pleasures (5:19b). Fourth, God gives gladness of heart (5:20).

The Teacher sees another life different from the one "under the sun." He has "seen it." It is enjoyable in toil, not in its absence. It is a God-given provision in a brief time of life. To eat and drink expresses companionship, joy, and satisfaction. These activities symbolize the peaceful contentment of a happy life. The Teacher encourages his readers to enjoy God's daily gifts. Instead of making riches the priority of life, we need to pursue God's gifts whether we are rich or poor.

Koheleth closes the section on money by stating the benefit of the godly way of living. "For they will scarcely brood over the days of their lives, because God keeps them occupied with the joy of their hearts" (5:20). Secular human beings may live a life of drudgery, but the God-centered person does not. Life will be so occupied with jubilation that the vanity of life will be forgotten.

The Teacher does not explicitly ask readers to make a choice, but he does imply one. He has presented two ways of life. One is the pursuit of wealth, which never satisfies and stays on earth after we die. He has presented another lifestyle for either the rich or the poor by enjoying God's gifts each day. The choice is obviously one between "brooding" and "enjoyment." "Brooding" means to experience emptiness, meaninglessness. It means a wallowing in dissatisfaction and emptiness. The choice seems to be obvious. But unfortunately some choose to be unhappy.

Chapter 8

The Sight of Disappointed People

6:1–12

In Koheleth's honest look at life, he sees the comprehensiveness of human existence. He views some people extremely contented, and he sees other people with deep disappointments. He described a contented person in 5:18–20 with the word "enjoyment" (5:18). It is a God-given provision. It is a word expressive of companionship, joy, and satisfaction. It is the symbol of a contented and happy life. The Teacher describes a person who acquired wealth and enjoyed it as a gift of God. But, beginning in 6:1, the Teacher views people who are greatly disappointed with life. Koheleth uses the word "evil" to describe this person's disappointment. This person has God's great gifts of wealth, possession, and honor. Yet this person lacked the ability to enjoy God's gifts. He lived in great disappointment.

Disappointment is not just a condition prevalent in Koheleth's day. It exists among all kinds of people and in every era of time. Only a casual look at life reveals the disappointments people have. Take a look in the schools: disappointment over a grade, over a performance on a test, over a careless word from a fellow student, or over not getting elected as president of the student body. Look in the business world: disappointment over low profits, over the lack of business, over a layoff or firing, over not getting promoted, or over not getting the raise other employees received. The sports world also has many disappointments: dropping the pass in a close game, not making the free throw to win the championship, not making the team, or losing the game. A look in numerous areas of life reveals people experiencing disappointment.

In Koheleth's observation of life, he saw the symptoms of disappointed people. Ecclesiastes 6 is one of the Bible's most depressing chapters. The point the Teacher makes is the possibility of possessing wealth, social position, a large family, and a long life without enjoying them. The writer sees a number of disappointments that left him greatly sad. The scenario in 6:1-12 describes a worse case than the two cases related earlier. In the two earlier cases, the toiler lived a dreary existence while hoarding wealth. Then, he lost it all (5:12-13), or he manages to hold on to his wealth but lived a joyless life (5:14-16). In Ecclesiastes 6 God lets a man have everything he wants, but he does not enjoy it. The chapter is a picture of disappointment: experiences without enjoyment (6:1-6), appetites without satisfaction (6:7-9), and advantage without adequacy (6:10-12).

Experiences without Enjoyment

6:1-6

The first disappointment Koheleth observes is people with possessions but not enjoying them. "There is an evil that I have seen under the sun, and it lies heavy upon humankind: those to whom God gives wealth, possessions, and honor, so that they lack nothing of all that they desire, yet God does not enable them to enjoy these things, but a stranger enjoys them. This is vanity; it is a grievous ill"(6:1-2). The Teacher observes a situation affecting human beings. He claims that many wealthy people cannot enjoy their experience with possessions. He labels the situation "an evil." He also described it as something that "lies heavy upon humankind." This person had the highly desirable assets of the ancient world, but he was still disappointed with life. He is rich and powerful, but because of his selfishness and greed, he lives with a sense of emptiness and disappointment.

The situation the Teacher introduced in 6:1 is now presented in 6:2. This person seems to have it all. Not only is he worth a fortune, but he is also famous. The Teacher used three words to describe the person: wealth, possessions, and honor. Yet for some unnamed reason this man is unable to enjoy his gifts from God. The Teacher says that one reason rich people might fail to enjoy their wealth is that a foreigner has taken it away from them. Apparently, the Teacher in verse 2 is thinking of a person who has no natural heirs and perhaps also dies young. The only people who can enjoy his wealth are people outside his family who by some legal process receive his wealth. In the ancient world to die without sons who would inherit one's possessions was considered a great tragedy. Consequently, for this man to work hard to attain wealth, possessions, and honor and never to enjoy them was a disappointing emptiness.[1] His life was filled with experiences but no enjoyment. Koheleth pronounces this predicament as meaningless.

The Teacher gives another strange reason this person was unable to enjoy his experiences with possessions. God does not enable this person to enjoy his daily gifts. Numerous attempts have been made to mitigate divine responsibility for the lack of enjoyment. The text reads, "God does not enable them to enjoy these things." The Teacher does not explain what he means by that statement. It could be that the writer did not recognize any secondary causes, and ultimately everything was caused by God. The enjoyment could have been caused by numerous situations within the person: greed, worry, self-centeredness, or no family to receive his inheritance.

The term "stranger" in verse 2 could have several applications. It could be sickness. Once the rich man had good health, but now a "stranger" attacked his body, and he can no longer enjoy the delights of fame and fortune. It could be a natural disaster. Earthquakes, floods, tornados, hurricanes, and other disasters could take away the rich person's wealth. Another "stranger" could be someone who stole the man possessions, and he watched others enjoy his wealth. The coming of a stranger happens frequently. One person loses everything he worked so hard to gain, but something or someone comes along to enjoy it. Such a world, viewed from the human perspective, seems to be "vanity and a grievous ill."

The Teacher moves in his observation to reflect more on the problem of people not being able to enjoy the experiences of God's gifts. The Teacher emphasizes that even if a person had one hundred children and lived an extremely long life, he may still be lacking in enjoyment. "A man may beget a hundred children, and live many years; but however many are the days of his years, if he does not enjoy life's good things, or has no burial, I say that a stillborn child is better off than he. For it comes into vanity and goes into darkness, and in darkness its name is covered; moreover it has not seen the sun or known anything; yet it finds rest rather than he" (6:3–5). The Teacher expands the theme of the person who has the resources to enjoy life but does not. In these verses the emphasis is not on the abundance of riches but on children and long life. Many Old Testament passages rejoice in large number of children (Ps. 127:4) and in long life (Prov. 3:2). Kohelth takes exception to these common teachings. He finds it conceivable that a person may be blessed with numerous children and a long life and still be absolutely miserable. The Teacher thinks the misery is so bad that a "stillborn child" has had a better life. The stillborn child exists momentarily but has no identity. According to Koheleth, the stillborn's fate is much preferred to the life of one who has been given riches, long life, and many children but not the ability to enjoy it all.[2]

The Teacher continues his description of the advantages of the stillborn child over the miserable rich. The stillborn child never sees the light of the sun. The stillborn child never reaches consciousness—"not knowing anything." This child never experiences the hardship and misery of life. Likewise, the child has "rest," unlike the rich who struggle continuously.[3]

Earlier the Teacher used a hyperbole in reference to the blessing of children. He also alluded to long life. Now he becomes more specific with a hyperbole about someone who lives two thousand years. "Even though he should have a thousand years twice over, yet enjoy no good—do not all go to the same place?" (6:6). Even though someone lives to this incredible old age, those years are meaningless if he is unable to enjoy them. Though two thousand years is a long time, even that life comes to a close with death. The enjoyment of life, according to the Teacher, is spoiled with death.[4] Sidney Geidanus captures the thought of Ecclesiastes 6:6, "To have lived so long and yet not to have enjoyed God's good gifts—what a waste."[5] In the thinking of Koheleth's day, one might have enjoyed life with lots of wealth, many children, and long life. But, none of these experiences brings enjoyment without God. It is a great disappointment.

Appetite without Satisfaction

6:7–9

The Teacher observes another angle about people's disappointments. They have numerous appetites, but they are never satisfied. The longings of the human heart cannot be satisfied with the experiences "under the sun." "All human toil is for the mouth, yet the appetite is not satisfied" (6:7). What does the Teacher mean by "mouth"? Probably the word refers to human cravings of all sorts, not just for food.[6]

The Hebrew word for "appetite" is *nephesh*. In other places in the Old Testament, translators render the word "soul." The inference could be that human beings have a craving in the soul or in one's deepest being that can never be satisfied with anything "under the sun."

Insatiable inner cravings characterize the human condition. "All human toil is for the mouth." In other words, we work in order to eat. Yet the appetite is never satisfied. After eating a large evening meal, we are hungry in the morning. Likewise, many human desires can never be satisfied. Think of some human cravings. When the desire for drink gets attention, the desire for drink returns. Sexual appetites never seem to be satisfied. Then there is the appetite for significance. Human beings desire to be somebody famous. They want to be noticed. Thus, they try to achieve, and as they earn accomplishments, the appetite continues.

Of course there is the human desire for wealth. The more possessions a person has, the more a person wants. No one has ever been able to determine how much money is "enough." Human beings can strive and strain for possessions, but the effort or accomplishments never afford them with soul satisfaction.

The Teacher asks two questions: Does a wise man have an advantage in this life? Does it help the poor man to ingratiate himself before others to improve his lot in life? "For what advantage have the wise over fools? And what do the poor have who know how to conduct themselves before the living" (6:8). One of the functions of wisdom, according to wisdom teaching, was to show the way to material riches. The wise would be blessed with wealth. Koheleth questioned this reasoning. The wise have no advantage in satisfying the desire for material goods. The poor, therefore, have no advantage in using wisdom. Perhaps wisdom could lead them to riches, but it could not satisfy the deepest desires of their souls.[7]

The Teacher closes this section with a proverb and a repetition of the hebel formula. "Better is the sight of the eyes than the wandering of desire; this also is vanity and a chasing after wind" (6:9). Koheleth compares the sight of the eyes to roving desires. The "wandering of desire" can never be satisfied. It is always wandering anxiously, seeking the satisfaction it cannot provide. Human desires are always traveling but never arriving.

"This also is vanity and a chasing after wind." The deepest human desires cannot be satisfied with earthly experiences. The Teacher seems to imply that human beings need God to satisfy the deepest desires of their souls. Trying to find satisfaction on earth—"under the sun"— brings great disappointment.

Advantages without Adequacy

6:10-12

Koheleth also observes that human beings have many advantages, but they are inadequate to cope with some circumstances and to answer many questions. They fail to recognize their finiteness and God's infiniteness. They fail to think of themselves as the creatures and God as the Creator. The Teacher begins his message with an identity of the human race in reference to God. "Whatever has come to be has already been named, and it is known what human beings are, and that they are not able to dispute with those who are stronger" (6:10). The concept of naming refers to God's naming things at creation: day, night, sky, earth, sea, etc. To give the name to a thing means to make it exist and to exercise control over it. Koheleth writes, "And it is known what human beings are." Human beings are known to be finite and weak. He refers to human limitations. They cannot escape some basic limitations.

Human beings are so limited "that they are not able to dispute with those who are stronger." The Hebrew reads "one who is stronger." The stronger one, of course, is God. He is the powerful Creator of the universe. He called all things into being. He named the creation. He called human beings into existence. It is futile to argue with God who is much stronger than mere humans.

The Teacher tells about the foolishness of a person disputing with God. "The more words, the more vanity, so how is one the better?" (6:11). Human beings need to know their identity—frail human beings who are creations of God. They do not have the wisdom to win an argument with God. Endless talking will not solve their problem or ultimately change things.

Koheleth uses two questions to close the section on advantages without adequacy. "For who knows what is good for mortals while they live the few days of their vain life, which they pass like a shadow?" (6:12a). This first question deals with human beings' present existence. "Who knows what is good for mortals?" Of course the implicit answer is, no one but God. No human beings know what is good for them. It is implied that they must acknowledge and accept what God gives them. The Teacher knows that life is like a shadow of a cloud crossing the sky. The years are vanity without God. The Teacher wants adequacy for the present.

The second question deals with the future. "For who can tell them what will be after them under the sun" (6:12b). The implied answer is, no one can tell human beings what will be after them. Koheleth seems to place the responsibility for what with happen in the future on God. Michael A. Eaton says the Teacher "is slamming every door except the door of faith."[8]

Disappointments prevailed in Koheleth's day. He observed many disappointed people. He saw the wealthy disappointed over the fact that they could not find enjoyment while they experienced their wealth. He saw people incessantly trying to satisfy the deep desire of the soul with earthly things and never getting satisfaction. He saw human beings disappointed that even though they had the advantages of being the crown of God's creation, they could not cope with a lot of the issues in life or answer some of the deepest questions of life. Maybe if we looked with the honesty and intensity of Koheleth, we might see the abundance of disappointed people.

Chapter 9

An Insight into What Is Good for People

7:1-8:1

Fortunately sometimes and unfortunately at other times chapter designations appear in English Bibles. These chapter markings help readers find places in Scripture. In most cases the chapter divisions correctly divide thoughts. But in some other cases, a chapter division may hinder the flow of thought. Such is the case between Ecclesiastes 6:10-12 and 7:1-8:1. There seems to be a vital link with the questions posed at the end of 6:12 and the material in Ecclesiastes chapter 7. "For who knows what is good for mortals?" and "Who can tell them what will be after them under the sun?" Evidently the author has graphically sketched the human predicament to show that there is something good for people. Notice the word "good." It leads to what follows in chapter 7, for then the author relates insight into what is "good" for people.

The Western mind wants logical, orderly progression in Bible books. Ecclesiastes, like all other books of the Bible, comes from the Semitic mind. Such a mind was not linear. Instead it was cyclic and repetitive. Westerners can profit in their study of Ecclesiastes by looking at a word or phrase repetition. Such repetitions help readers see a unifying theme of a section and how thought blocks in the section relate to the theme or the repetitive word or phrase. The word wise/wisdom appears fourteen times in 7:1–8:1; therefore, the unifying theme is "wisdom." Koheleth sees that wisdom is really what is good for people. In times of human adversity, wisdom can bring some good. Koheleth presents four thought blocks stacked around the concept of wisdom.

The Teachableness of Wisdom

7:1–6

The Teacher begins by telling his readers that wisdom can detect some good even in times of adversity. He gives a series of proverbs that repeat the words "good" and "better than." Verse 1 contains a proverb in two parts. The first part contains a play on words (shem—name; shemen—ointment). He begins with a rather traditional statement. "A good name is better than precious ointment" (7:1a). Traditional wisdom valued highly a person's reputation. The writer of Proverbs wrote, "A good name is to be chosen rather than great riches" (Prov.

22:1a). One can purchase precious ointment, but no one can buy a good reputation.

The second half of verse 1 presents an abrupt contrast to the first half of the verse. Derek Kidner writes, "Nothing is the first half of verse 1 prepares us for the body blow of the second half."[1] The Teacher says in the last half of verse 1, "the day of death, than the day of birth"(7:1b). He says that the day one dies is better than the day one is born. The day of birth begins the lifetime of witnessing the oppressed and being oppressed. But the day of death marks the end of seeing the suffering of others and of one's own suffering.

Koheleth continues the theme of death. "It is better to go to the house of mourning than to go to the house of feasting; for this is the end of everyone, and the living will lay it to heart" (7:2). The Teacher thinks it is better to attend a funeral than a wedding reception. Why does the Teacher say such a thing? Going to the house of mourning causes us to think seriously about death. Ernest Becker in The *Denial of Death* writes, "The day of death, the fear of it, haunts the human animal like nothing else."[2] We attempt to avoid the morbid talk of death. We would prefer denial. But when we go to the house of mourning, we can no longer deny the reality of death. The visit reminds us. "I, too, will die one day." The living will keep the reality of death in their heart—"the living will lay it to heart."

Wisdom teaches human beings in unique ways. It has a way of reversing our likes and dislikes. "Sorrow is better than laughter, for by sadness of countenance the heart is made glad" (7:3). The Teacher does not mean the enjoyment of life he recommends throughout the book. He uses the word "laughter" to mean "to behave in a frivolous manner."[3] The serious countenance communicates the person's mind. Wisdom is that strange teacher who helps us learn and profit in sorrow rather than frivolity. The discipline of sorrow leads to a realistic appraisal of life which brings happiness while the excesses of mirth or gaiety lead to unhappiness.

Koheleth repeats the thought of going to the house of mourning, which he mentioned in verse 2. "The heart of the wise is in the house of mourning, but the heart of fools is in the house of mirth" (7:4). He states again that the wise person contemplates his or her ultimate death, but the fool lives blithely as if there was no end. Sidney Greidanus writes, "Perhaps the wild parties in the house of mirth will drown out the thoughts of death."[4]

Koheleth now moves away from the idea of death and mourning to a contrast between wisdom and folly. "It is better to hear the rebuke of the wise than to hear the song of fools. For the crackling of thorns under a pot, so is the laughter of fools, this also is vanity" (7:5-6). The Teacher is not impressed by the song of fools or by their laughter. The pun "crackling of thorns" pictures the passing nature of the fool's laughter. Thorns burned rapidly. Thus, fools' laughter is a sudden flame, a sudden display of fire, accompanied for plenty of noise, but soon they burn out.[5] The Teacher thinks the fool's laughter is vanity. It is short-lived.

Koheleth wants his readers to think about what is good for them. Most people do not value sorrow, pain, bereavements, and disappointments of life. But these circumstances can teach us the most when we apply God's wisdom to them. By being in tough situations, we can become stronger and equipped to cope with life. The Teacher advises his readers to approach the realistic, tough times wisely. It is not wise to deny that tough times exist. It is not wise to run away from them. It is not wise to protest angrily against them. It is not wise to laugh them off. Wisdom teaches us to face them, reflect on them, and see how they can help us. In this way the tough times can be good.[6]

The Threats to Wisdom

7:7–9

Wisdom does not make a person completely safe. Threats come to the wise person that can cause them to act unwisely. "Surely oppression make the wise foolish, and a bribe corrupts the heart" (7:7). The Teacher specifically mentions "oppression" and a "bribe." Both of these, oppression and bribery, weaken wisdom. They present such a threat to the wise, that the wise could yield to one or both and become foolish.

The Teacher uncovers the effect of a bribe on one's judgment. The wise person can become a fool when money is involved. Wisdom is weakened by extortion, on the one hand, and bribery on the other. Extortion requires payment from someone in return for silence, and bribery is the receipt of money in return for some desired action. Extortion makes the wise person a fool by giving control of life to another. Bribery clouds one's judgment by introducing bias.[7] The wise person who joins the pursuit of possessions, compromising integrity in the process, becomes just as much a fool as the wise person who joins with fools in empty laughter.[8]

Not only do extortion and bribery sidetrack the wise, but also impatience sidetracks the wise. "Better is the end of a thing than its beginning; the patient in spirit are better than the proud in spirit" (7:8). The Teacher has a world for those wanting instant results. He uses a proverb of "better than" to make a comparison. We are so accustomed to getting quick results that we are losing the ability to endure. Unless we can see the results immediately, we do not stay with it. The "end of a thing" means the "outcome," the "end product." The proverb implies that times of testing may be purposeful, that they are confined to limited seasons, and the results make them worthwhile. The Teacher wants his readers to grasp the hope of a trial and to face it accordingly. This will prevent premature complaints, boasting, or arrogance and thus be "patient in spirit" rather than "proud in spirit."

Closely akin to impatience is anger. Koheleth warns about anger being a threat to wisdom. "Do not be quick to anger, for anger lodges in the bosom of fools" (7:9). Fools do not have patience. They quickly explode over an issue that disturbs them. When life does not go their way, they respond with anger. The Teacher says that anger "lodges in the bosom of fools." The fool coddles anger, nurtures it, and allows it to grow. Then ultimately the anger explodes outwardly in unkind words or actions. If tolerated, anger makes a home in the personality of the fool. The term "bosom" indicates the innermost part of a person. Since anger is the quality of a fool, if a wise person acts in anger, he acts like a fool. The Teacher advocates a calm attitude for life. Wise people do not react immediately to circumstances. Instead, they take a long-term view, waiting to see the full picture before deciding how to respond. Fools arrogantly and angrily make a knee-jerk response.[9]

The Teacher's mention of the last threat to wisdom is nostalgia. He counters the glorifying of the past at the expense of the present. "Do not say, 'Why were the former days better than these?' For it is not from wisdom that you ask this" (7:10). Koheleth evidently quotes a saying common in his day. People voice a preference for the past. The rapid changes culturally and economically influence a nostalgic longing for the past. The question, "Why were the former days better than these?" comes across as a lament of the present. To devalue the present in favor of the past is anathema to Koheleth. Of course he is not saying that the present is an improvement over the past. Rather, he addresses people thinking of the past to escape the challenge of the present. The immediate constitutes life from which no one can or should try to escape. Brown writes, "Wisdom informs the living of these days, not the reliving of the 'former days.'"[10]

Wisdom has its threats. Extortion is an escape from responsibility. Impatience gives in too early and is short on reality. Anger places the fault in everyone else and causes hateful attitudes and actions. Nostalgia seeks to escape to a former time and not take responsibility for the present. These threats and others can lead the wise person to think or to act foolishly.

The Value of Wisdom

7:11-18

Having warned of the threats to wisdom, the Teacher now moves to discussing the advantages of wisdom. What does the Teacher mean by wisdom? In some cases the Teacher uses wisdom in the sense of secular knowledge. That seems to be the case in most uses of the word wisdom in Ecclesiastes chapters 1-6. This secular wisdom could refer to academic prowess. Koheleth seems to use the word wisdom in the last section of Ecclesiastes (chap. 7-12) as reverent living before God. It is to fear God above everything else. It means to understand life "under the sun" from God's viewpoint. It means to reflect prudently on one's experience from the perspective of divine revelation. Godly wisdom, not secular wisdom, is better for humans to have. Wisdom is what is good for mortals to have while they live their few days of life on earth.

The Teacher underscores the value of this godly wisdom. "Wisdom is as good as an inheritance, an advantage to those who see the sun" (7:11). The combination of wisdom with and inheritance benefits those who see the sun. The word "inheritance" could have meant the land. God gave Israel the land of Canaan, and it was apportioned for inheritance (Num. 26:53). Each family except the Levites received a portion of the land. This land passes on from father to son or daughter to remain in the family. The land symbolized a permanent possession. It yielded food, so it meant security and provision. The expression "to those who see the sun" refers to those who are living. Wisdom guides and protects them with money as long as they live life on earth.

In describing the value of wisdom, Koheleth compares the protection of wisdom to the protection of possessions. "For the protection of wisdom is like the protection of money, and the advantage of knowledge is that wisdom gives life to the one who possesses it" (7:12). Money can, to some extent, protect people from hardship. It can safeguard against hunger. It can provide shelter and clothes to wear. Likewise, wisdom can protect people from the hard realities of life.

Of course wisdom has a great advantage over possessions. "And the advantage of knowledge is that wisdom gives life to the one who possesses it." The Teacher praises wisdom and possessions, but he gives wisdom the most favorable position. Wisdom gives a greater life to the person who possesses it. Money by itself does not give the higher life.

Another value of wisdom is that it helps to keep God in consideration. "Consider the work of God; who can make straight what he has made crooked?" (7:13). Koheleth urges listeners to be attentive to the work of God in the world. The term "crooked" probably refers to sorrow, mourning, and death in the world. Derek Kidner does not think "crooked" refers to moral problems but "the shape of things and events which we find awkward but should accept from God."[11] No one can make straight the events life brings. Human beings have no choice but to accept the awkward things in life that cannot be changed.

Wisdom leads people to accept what cannot be changed. "In the day of prosperity be joyful, and in the day of adversity consider; God has made the one as well as the other, so that mortals may not find out anything that will come after them" (7:14). Old Testament writers did not think of secondary causes. They saw God as the primary cause of everything, good or bad. God has made both the day of prosperity and the day of adversity. Humans can do nothing but accept the good of prosperity as well as the bad of adversity as it comes from the hand of God. No one knows what the future holds. Wisdom teaches people to trust in the God who controls the future.

The Paradox of Wisdom

7:15–22

The Teacher continues his insight on wisdom with a major puzzle that confronts all of us. He writes, "In my vain life I have seen everything; there are righteous people who perish in their righteousness, and there are wicked people who prolong their life in evildoing" (7:15). Koheleth has lived long enough to observe that some righteous people die young while some wicked people grow old. He sees good people suffer and evil people thriving. Harold Kushner has caused a lot of people to think about this paradox in his book *When Bad Things Happen to Good People*. He writes about his young son Aaron who had a rapid-aging disease and died young. He died before he had time to become evil. Such an experience does not match with traditional thinking that the good get good things and the evil bad things.

Seeing the paradox of the righteous suffering and the wicked prospering does not just belong to Koheleth's day. It belongs to our day in hundreds and hundreds of incidents: a young wife and mother dedicated to the Lord dies early from breast cancer; a seminary student with passionate plans to be a pastor dies in a car accident; an eight-year-old child dies from leukemia. Meanwhile, hundreds and hundreds of incidents happen the opposite way: a man unfaithful to his wife for many, many years lives to an old age; a sex offender enjoys the benefit of Social Security and retirement; a mass murderer lives in prison for decades. It does not seem right. How can God allow the travesty of such justice?

Koheleth discusses the paradox he has presented in an unusual manner. "Do not be too righteous, and do not act too wise; why should you destroy yourself? Do not be too wicked, and do not be a fool; why should you die before your time?" (7:16–17). What does Koheleth mean by being "too righteous" or "too wicked"? Perhaps he thought of God's promise of long life to the righteous. Some of the Teacher's readers might have thought that those people who died young were not righteous enough. Therefore, they think they must pursue more righteousness in order to prolong life. Maybe the Teacher intends to warn against an overpious attitude, on one hand, and its opposite, an antinomian disdain of the law, on the other.

The Teacher responds to his readers' thinking by advising, "Do not be too righteous. . . . Do not be too wicked." The Teacher rejects overconfidence in righteousness and wisdom. He warns against the notion that it is possible for one to be so righteous that he or she could avert destruction and extend life. No matter how righteous we become, we can never force God to extend our lives because of our righteousness.

The Teacher also adds, "Do not act too wisely." People should not pursue wisdom "hoping to gain an edge over God and force his hand."[12] The pursuit of being righteous and wise raises the question, "Why should you destroy yourself?" Those who think they can become super righteous or super wise are headed for destruction. "Pride goes before destruction, and a haughty spirit before a fall" (Prov. 16:18).

After thinking about being "too righteous," the Teacher turns to the idea of being "too wicked." He warns not to choose to be wicked or to sin deliberately. More than likely that kind of lifestyle could lead to an early death. Everyone sins inevitably, but those who embrace an evil way of life are destroyed by it.

Koheleth makes a recommendation for such a paradox of the righteous dying young and the evil living long. "It is good that you take hold of the one, without letting go of the other; for the one who fears God shall succeed with both"(7:18). What does the Teacher mean by "the one" and the "other"? Previously, he has observed that good people suffer and bad people thrive. He recommends a middle-of-the-road approach to life that is not too self-serving about righteousness and wisdom or too foolish about wickedness. He thinks that one who "fears" God will choose a middle stance between the two extremes.

Ecclesiastes 7:19–20 seems to be a parenthesis on wisdom or two verses that belong with 7:12. This writer thinks this verse represents a parenthesis more than a text moved from its original place. Koheleth gives an insertion that wisdom is much more important than any human qualities and abilities. "Wisdom gives strength to the wise more than ten rulers that are in a city" (7:19). We think of political rulers as the most important and powerful people in a city. They make decisions which affect a large number of people. Their decision can mean wealth or poverty, sickness or health, life or death. Koheleth states that one single wise person is stronger than ten city officials. The ten-to-one ratio probably is a hyperbole.

But Koheleth does not want his readers to think that wisdom is perfect. "Surely there is no one on earth so righteous as to do good without ever sinning" (7:20). Even the extremely wise and extremely righteous person sins. The Teacher continues by giving an example of the universality of sin. "Do not give heed to everything that people say, or you may hear your servant cursing you; your heart knows that many times you have yourself cursed others" (7:21–22). If one listens to what others say, he or she will never be at peace. You know people say things about you behind your back because you have done the same to others.

The Inaccessibility of Wisdom

7:23–8:1

The Teacher wanted to understand why some good people die young while some bad people die old. Though Koheleth knows the limitation of wisdom in general and his ability to achieve it in particular, he nonetheless expresses his desire to pursue it. "All this I have tested by wisdom; I said, 'I will be wise,' but it was far from me" (7:23). Though Koheleth had the determination to get wisdom, he found it far from him.

Why was this wisdom beyond the reach of the Teacher? "That which is, is far off, and deep, very deep; who can find it out?" (7:24) The Teacher sees "that which is"—the puzzling, paradoxical realities in life. "That which is, is far off, and deep, very deep." Koheleth sees the problem to be both horizontal and vertical. To see "far away" means not seeing an end in sight. To say "deep, very deep" means not being able to fathom the depths. It is beyond human understanding why God allows life to happen the way it does.

The Teacher would not give up in his search for wisdom. "I turned my mind to know and to search out and to seek wisdom and the sum of things, and to know that wickedness is folly and that foolishness is madness" (7:25). The verbs "search," "seek," and "know" express Koheleth's passion in his pursuit. What is the object of Koheleth's search? He names "wisdom" and "the sum of things." He also seeks to know "that wickedness is folly and that foolishness is madness." He wanted to know wisdom so he could make sense of life. He wanted to know why wickedness even exists and how it fits into God's world.

After announcing his intention to search things out, the Teacher reports on his discoveries. He uses the word "found" four times, indicating the four discoveries he made (7:26, 27, 28, 29). First, he discovered the alluring wickedness of the world. "I found more bitter than death the woman who is a trap, whose heart is snares and nets, whose hands are fetters; one who pleases God escapes her, the sinner is taken by her" (7:26). Koheleth does not speak of women in general, only a particular kind of woman. Only the wicked woman is more bitter than death. The evil woman's personality is dominated by the instincts of the hunter (snares and nets), and she is forceful in her hold, binding victims so that no escape is possible.

Koheleth gives the results of being attracted by evil. On one hand the person who pleases God escapes the wicked woman. But, on the other hand, the sinner is taken by her.

Second, Koheleth gives another discovery. He could not find the reason for all things. "See, this is what I found, says the Teacher, adding one thing to another to find the sum, which my mind has sought repeatedly, but I have not found" (7:27-28). He found righteous people who perished early in life, and he found wicked people doing evil for many years. He found wickedness that destroyed all but those who please God. "But I have not found" the sum of things. He lives in a paradoxical world where bad things happen to good people.

Third, Koheleth could scarcely find an upright person. "One man among a thousand I found, but a woman among all these I have not found" (7:28b). Koheleth's words have stirred strong debate. Many attempts have been made to soften the misogynistic tone. Some think the Teacher condemns only those women who fit the description in 7:26. On the surface Koheleth seems to make an uncomplimentary remark about humanity in general and women in particular. Koheleth did express himself as a misogynist in verse 28. In other places he speaks favorably of women (9:9). The view of Koheleth is not the teachings of the book of Ecclesiastes any more that the speeches of the three friends constitute normative teaching of the book of Job.[13] Michael Fox suggests that the Teacher might have intended this remark "as a wisecrack rather than a solemn statement."[14] Probably Koheleth used hyperbole and reports only "one upright man among a thousand but not one upright woman among them." Whether the Teacher quotes a proverb or composes one himself, his point is that he has found virtually no upright persons.[15]

The fourth discovery Koheleth makes is that God made all human beings upright. "See, this alone I found, that God made human beings straightforward, but they have devised many schemes" (7:29). This discovery covers everything Koheleth discovered. He is driven to a single point that is the source of calamities previously described (vs. 15-28). The blame for the rarity of wisdom is attributed to no one but human beings. They were created "straightforward," which means a state of the heart which is to be disposed to faithfulness or obedience. Human beings devised many schemes that have led to pain, suffering, and death. "This I found" shows that Koheleth's theology was confirmed by life itself.

The Teacher closes with a praise of wisdom. "Who is like the wise man? And who knows the interpretation of a thing?" (8:1a) He praises wisdom for helping people survive in a dangerous, unjust world. He asks, "Who is the wise man?" The expected answer is, no one. The Teacher follows with a second question, "And who knows the interpretation of a thing?" Again the expected answer is, no one. The word "interpretation" is used in Genesis 40:5 for the interpretation of dreams. Where, asks the Teacher, can you find a person who discerns ways through the problems of life: The person with godly wisdom interprets correctly the mysteries of providence.[16]

Koheleth's final praise of wisdom is what it does to a person's countenance. "Wisdom makes one's face shine, and the hardness of one's countenance is changed" (8:1b). The face reflects the inner feelings of a person. The shining face indicates contentment of heart. The presence of wisdom can be seen on a person's face.

Koheleth answered the question, "For who knows what is good for mortals?" His answer may be summarized in one word, "Wisdom." That kind of wisdom differs from human reasoning under the sun. This wisdom comes from God.

Chapter 10

A Reflection about Coping with Some Difficulties in Life

8:2-17

Scott Peck opens his popular book with the statement: "Life is difficult."[1] All of us know this assertion is true. Everyone experiences the problems and puzzles of life. Some encounter more difficulties that others. For example, many people in the world struggle with years of illness. Others cope with some type of physical or mental handicap all of their lives. Many people struggle with debilitating depression, annoying anxieties, or some other emotional difficulty. Numerous persons suffer from poverty, abusive relationships, and other injustices. Life, even at its best, involves many difficult situations.

Koheleth has been taking an honest look at life in Ecclesiastes 1–6. Periodically, the Teacher reported life to be *hebel*—"vanity," "absurd," "meaningless." In many different ways Koheleth has asserted life to be difficult. Listening to Koheleth's insights about life could lead us to characterize him as a pessimist or a nihilist. Instead of being a pessimist or a nihilist, he is a realist. He takes an honest look at life. But, even in his true-to-life observations, he implicitly expressed the truth that life is difficult.

After the midpoint of Ecclesiastes, readers begin to notice that the Teacher was not a pure pessimist about life. Beginning in 7:1 he turns from realistic observations about life to practical considerations about how to cope with life. Previously in chapters 1–6 the Teacher has portrayed some difficulties, puzzles, and predicaments in order to show his readers how wisdom can detect some good even in times of difficulty (7:1–8:1). While many of the situations of life cannot be changed, wisdom can be the resource to help with difficult situations.

Beginning in chapter 8 the Teacher mentions several specific difficulties people encounter in life. He continues with the inferred need for wisdom in these hard situations. In chapter 8 Koheleth gives some reflections about how people can cope with some difficulties of life. The Teacher records his difficulties with life in chapters 1–6 and moves to a more helpful note in 7:1–8:1 with the praise of wisdom. Then in 8:2–17 the Teacher offers some pragmatic suggestions about how to use the wisdom in four challenges of life.

Difficulty with Allegiance to Authority

8:2-5

The Teacher first mentions the difficulty people have in dealing with authority. He talks of the king. We would not speak of the king but of the government. The Teacher's insights could relate to the government or apply to any person or organization with authority over us. Submitting to authority is a difficult situation. Koheleth begins his practical reflections by telling how to exercise wisdom in our submission to authority. He gives practical guidance for dealing with earthly governments, whether good or bad. "Keep the king's command because of your sacred oath" (8:2). A wise citizen will do what the king says. There seems to be an excellent reason to obey the king—"because of your sacred oath." The sacred oath is the vow a king's citizens take to be loyal to the king. The Teacher reminds readers that they have promised to obey the king.

God ordained physical laws to provide the universe with coherence. He also planned governments to provide coherence in society, to enable human beings with reasonable restraint, and to permit good to prevail. Since God has ordained governments, our attitude to them says something about our attitude toward God.

The Teacher proceeds in verse 3 to expand on a person's

allegiance to government authority. We may wish to disagree vigorously with some policies and decisions. It may seem best to withdraw our support from the particular government or even engage in disloyal rebellious action. The Teacher gives a word of caution: "Do not be terrified; go from his presence, do not delay when the matter is unpleasant, for he does whatever he pleases" (8:3). He is not accountable to any other human being.[2] "For the word of the king is powerful, and who can say to him, 'What are you doing?'" (8:4). It would be fruitless, even dangerous to question his actions. The better decision is just to obey whatever he says. According to Derek Kidner, there are times when "wisdom has to fold its wings and take the form of discretion, content to keep its possessor out of trouble."[3]

The Teacher goes on to teach that the wise person will know the right things to do and the right time to speak. "Whoever obeys a command will meet no harm, and the wise man will know the time and way" (8:5). The Teacher is not a coward who says we are to take everything the king passes our way, no matter what. He is not indifferent to justice. He simply advises that when misery weighs heavily upon people, they need to pick the moment to stand against injustice and protest with care. The wise person will have the appropriate time to act and the proper way to protest. Koheleth gives a typical wisdom admonition of appropriate timing in action and word.

Difficulty with Human Helplessness

8:6–9

The Teacher recognizes that there are many situations over which a person has no power. So the Teacher takes some time to discuss the difficulty of human helplessness. In 8:5 Koheleth described the wise person as one who knows "the time and way." While he affirms that there is a time and custom for everything, he states that it is of no real value to anyone. Human beings are beset with trouble unable to know what the future will bring. "Indeed, they do not know what is to be, for who can tell them how it will be?" (8:7). Though there is a "right time" for everything, that time is known only by God. He has concealed it from his creatures. They cannot control the future. They must comply with human limitation.

The Teacher emphasizes human limitations with a question, "Who can tell them how it will be?" Regarding the future, we can find help neither in ourselves nor from anyone else. Koheleth moves in his discussion to cite four instances of human impotence. "No one has power over the wind to restrain the wind, or power over the day of death; there is no discharge from the battle, nor does wickedness deliver those who practice it" (8:8). First, no one has power over the wind. Those who have experienced hurricanes or tornadoes know the feeling of helplessness. No one has power to control the wind.

Second, no one has power over the day of death. That experience seems to be in God's appointed time. Medical technology may postpone death, but it ultimately will come.

Third, no one has the power to discharge themselves from battle. Once the battle starts, no one can select a substitute and send them to battle in their place. Fourth, just as those involved in warfare cannot escape from it, so also will those involved in doing evil. They cannot escape the ultimate consequence of their evil. Koheleth in this example seems to believe in divine judgment.[4]

Koheleth concludes his ideas of human helplessness by giving a summary statement: "All this I observed, applying my mind to all that is done under the sun, while one person exercises authority over another to the other's hurt" (8:9). The Teacher advised strongly to use wisdom to cope with a difficult world. They had better use wisdom to escape the wrath of a fickle king. But he also observed that wisdom has its limitations. No human being knows what the future holds. They do not know when tragedies will strike. They cannot restrain the wind, change the day of death, discharge themselves from battle, or escape the power of wickedness. The Teacher acknowledges the pervasiveness of oppression "under the sun." There seems to be no one who can act on behalf of the powerless. Because of this lack of power, Koheleth advocates compliance before powerful people. To do otherwise would be dangerously imprudent. Resistance will prove to be destructive.

Difficulty with Traditional Theology

8:10-15

Throughout the book of Ecclesiastes, Koheleth deals with the difficulty of traditional theology. His honesty often gets him the label of being a liberal or an agnostic. Of course traditional theology is not always biblical theology. Numerous ideas exist about God's nature and work that do not have biblical support. Traditional theology is a thinking about God that comes from cultural influences, pure human reasoning, perpetuation of long-held traditions, or faulty biblical exegesis. Previously, the Teacher has gone against the traditional theology that good things happed to good people and bad things happen to bad people. He came out against long life being a sign of goodness and brevity as a sign of evil. These traditional theological ideas and many others gave Koheleth deep trouble.

In 8:10-15 the Teacher confronts the traditional theological concept of divine retribution. Are the wicked punished or not? From the Teacher's viewpoint in 8:10-12a it does not seem they are. Wickedness seems to thrive because there is no apparent punishment for it. Thankfully, Kohelth was not one who had arrived in his theological axioms, but he represents a person in process. As he continues to reason and to think, he seems to change his mind about divine retribution in 10:12–13. In these verses he seems to conclude that the wicked will be punished.

The Teacher shares with readers some of his theological reasoning process. He explores the sight of injustice in the world. "Then I saw the wicked buried; they used to go in and out of the holy place, and were praised in the city where they had done such things. This also is vanity" (8:10). Koheleth observes the burial of the wicked. Though the good and bad both die, the wicked seem to have it better in death. They are honored with a proper burial. They are even praised in the city despite their evil deeds. "This also is vanity," says the Teacher. It just does not make any sense. It is absurd. On the surface it seems as if it pays to be wicked. They ultimately died like everyone else, but they seem to be honored with a proper burial. Even though they were evil, they used to go in and out of the holy place. They were honored with a funeral. Furthermore, they were praised in the city where they did their evil deeds. The Teacher assesses this as "vanity." It does not make sense. It is absurd. It seems as if it pays to be evil. The wicked receive the praise owed to the righteous, and Koheleth utters his frustration about such senselessness.

The absence of retribution was at the heart of the Teacher's frustration. He now formulates the problem and states why it is a problem. "Because sentence against an evil deed is not executed speedily, the human heart is fully set to do evil" (8:11). He asserts that if there is no punishment for evil, then it will flourish. If people do not see the negative consequences of evil actions, they will be motivated to do even more evil.[5] The lack of a hasty and just punishment is enough to encourage evil people to plan new evil ways.

The Teacher continues his problem about retribution by recognizing that some extremely evil people live a long time. Traditionally, a long life was considered to be a result of God's blessing (Prov. 3:2, 16, 18). "Though sinners do evil a hundred times and prolong their lives, yet I know that it will be well with those who fear God, because they stand in fear before him" (8:12). Usually the Teacher tells us something he "saw," but now he tells us something he "knows." The Teacher seems to be content to wait patiently. The sinner may be great (a hundred times) and his life prolonged, but the Teacher holds it as a matter of faith that the vindication of the righteous is only a matter of time. He states that things will go well for those who fear God. "Yet I know that it will be well with those who fear God."

Koheleth contradicts what he stated in the first part of 8:12a and continues with what he started in 8:12b. "But it will not be well with the wicked, neither will they prolong their days like a shadow, because they do not stand in fear before God" (8:13). In 8:12a he expressed his frustration that the wicked lived a long time. In 8:13 he states that the wicked will not live a long time. Michael Eaton thinks the Teacher intentionally put the two statements side by side to be deliberately provocative. From his "under the sun" viewpoint the Teacher is infuriated in the long-term survival of the wicked. From the perspective of faith, things look different. The Teacher cannot imagine sin endlessly unrebuked and unjudged.[6]

Koheleth returns to the theme of retribution, which he introduced in 8:10. No one gets what he deserves! The righteous do not get rewarded; they get punished. The wicked do not get punished; they get rewarded. Once again Koheleth takes the reader back to the teaching of 8:10-12a. 'There is a vanity that takes place on earth, that there are righteous people who are treated according to the conduct of the wicked, and there are wicked people who are treated according to the conduct of the righteous. I said that this also is vanity" (8:14). To treat the righteous and the wicked according to what they deserve would mean that the righteous would die old and the wicked would die young. But Koheleth did not observe this as a reality in life. He again expresses his frustration that the situation is meaningless.

Faced with the enigma, Koheleth goes back to some earlier advice. "So I commend enjoyment, for there is nothing better for people under the sun than to eat, and drink, and enjoy themselves, for this will go with them in their toil through the days of life that God gives them under the sun" (8:15). The Teacher recommends the pleasure of eating and drinking in light of the meaningless existence. In spite of the injustices of the world and in spite of the puzzling questions about fairness, wise people seek to enjoy themselves with the life God gives them.

With each carpe diem passage, Koheleth speaks with increasing confidence. He uses "I commend" before the characteristic expression "there is nothing better." This advice is not new. He offered it previously (2:24, 25; 3:12–13, 22 and 5:18–20). The Teacher recognizes that pleasures do not have any ultimate answers, but he is convicted that enjoying God's gifts is important to people struggling with the meaning and mysteries of life and God.

Difficulty with the Recognition of Reality

8:16–17

The Teacher moves next to the difficulty of finding meaning for human existence. Koheleth shares his obsessive search for life's meaning. He has spent numerous days and many sleepless nights in his quest. But he finally concludes with the reality that human beings cannot find the ultimate answers of life. "When I applied my mind to know wisdom, and to see the business that is done on earth, how one's eyes see sleep neither day nor night, then I saw all the work of God, that no one can find out what is happening under the sun" (8:16-17a).

In Koheleth's final statements in verses 16 and 17 about coping with life in a difficult world, he uses the same expression three times—"no one can find it." In spite of hard work, no one can figure out what God is up to in his universe. Not even the wise man can understand the work of God. "However much they may toil in seeking, they will not find it out; even though those who are wise claim to know, they will not find it out" (8:17b). Contradiction rules in all of the experiences of life.

Aarre Lauha sees the answer to the Teacher's frustration in divine revelation. God revealed himself accurately but not fully during the Old Testament period. Lauha adds, "History, nature, and cult are all silent in regard accord to him."[7] Despite all of the human efforts to find out the meaning of life, human beings cannot discover its meaning. Partial answers can be given. Tentative solutions may be offered. But an arrogant and unfeeling fool would claim to know everything about suffering or injustice of the other enigmas of life. Life under the sun will always be like a jigsaw puzzle with some of the pieces missing. The missing pieces need not make us anxious, for we know in whose hands these pieces are to be found.

Koheleth's skeptical view of getting theological knowledge should, if anything, give people of faith pause for thought. That "the Lord works in mysterious ways" is not an empty cliché for the Teacher. Mystery is natural to God. Life "under the sun" is also fraught with mystery. Time itself is structured with polarities. God has made the day of peace and the day of adversity. The incessant oscillations between the good and the bad that make up what is "done under the sun" act to veil God's intention and purpose from all human perception and knowledge. God is in heaven, and we are upon the earth (cf. Eccl. 5:2). A great gulf divides the Transcendence from human finiteness. Koheleth's theology leads to a humble confession of humanity's finitude and limited discernment, a bitter pill that even the wisest of the wise must swallow.[8]

Both reading Ecclesiastes and living our lives will yield the conclusion that life is difficult. Does Koheleth advise us? "Just give up." "Don't worry with all that stuff about life and its adversities." No, he encourages by his example to keep searching and seeking for life's meaning throughout numerous painful days and many sleepless nights. The searching and seeking may make us resemble a person called Koheleth who struggled endlessly to find an ultimate satisfying meaning to life.

Chapter 11

An Honest, Last Look at Life

9:1–18

My wife wanted to read a book I had just read. She started reading the book, but I noticed before she got even to a fourth of the book she quit. I waited several days to see if she would resume reading the book, but she did not. I asked her, "How do you like the book?" She replied, "It's terrible! I cannot stand to read about the kidnap of a little girl with the fear of what might happen to her. The book is depressing, and it makes me sad." I encouraged her to keep reading, "The book will get better." She reluctantly kept reading, and she noticed a drastic turn in the story. Other than the tragic incident at the beginning, my wife loved the book. This tragic incident led her to read of many interesting and unique insights into theology.

Perhaps many readers want to quit Ecclesiastes by chapter 6 and certainly by chapter 8. It may be ruthlessly realistic, and, for many, it dwells too much on the emptiness and problems of life. Those who are not depressed before reading the first eight chapters of Ecclesiastes will be after reading them. Readers think by this point in their reading, life is a puff of wind, zilch, nothing, vanity, meaninglessness, insignificant, absurd, chasing after the wind. Let me urge you to stay with your reading and studying of Ecclesiastes until the book ends. You will notice that a turning point takes place after chapter 9. After chapter 9, the Teacher becomes more positive and optimistic. But, before he becomes more positive, he does take one last lingering look at the frustrations of life and dwells again on the frustration of the reality of death.

James Crenshaw writes, "A lengthening shadow extended throughout the book, becoming especially dark in this unit" (9:1-18).[1] The Teacher in chapters 7 and 8 has struggled with why bad things happen to some good people and why good things happen to some bad people. How can life be fair? How can God allow these circumstances to happen? The Teacher ended chapter 8 with the conclusion "no one can find out." Then Koheleth takes a turn with the words, "All this I laid to heart" (9:1a). Once again he will turn to the thought that people do not automatically get what they deserve. In fact the possibility exists that they may get the opposite of what they deserve. This opening line of chapter 9 marks Koheleth's attempt to analyze the fullness of his observations and experiences. To lay "to heart" means the seat of intelligence and will in Hebrew thought. The Teacher takes one last honest, intellectual attempt to look at life.

Life's Similar Experiences

9:1-3

Koheleth begins this honest look at life by declaring that God determines the character and conduct of the righteous. "All this I laid to heart, examining it all, how the righteous and the wise and their deeds are in the hands of God; whether it is love or hate one does not know" (9:1a). When good people suffer, observers have conflicting thoughts about whether the victims are in the "hands of God" or in his care. The problem according to the Teacher is that the righteous and the wise do not know whether what they experience is a result of God's love or his displeasure. Koheleth thinks that what people experience in life does not conclude whether God is pleased or displeased. The rationale behind love or hatred cannot be fathomable to human beings.

Both the righteous and the wicked have the same experiences in life. When rain comes, the righteous as well as the wicked get flooded If there is an earthquake, both of their houses fall. If there is an economic depression, both go broke. The Teacher realized that the righteous and the wicked could not be separated on the basis of what happens in the world. It is absolutely impossible to determine who has and who does not have God's favor.[2]

In Koheleth's serious thinking, he concludes that life is futile because regardless of what one does or is, the same consequences happen. He lists several examples of extremes to underscore the absurdity of it all. "Everything that confronts them is vanity, since the same fate comes to all, to the righteous and the wicked, to the good and the evil, to the clean and the unclean, to those who sacrifice and those who do not sacrifice. As are the good, so are the sinners; those who swear are like those who shun an oath" (9:1b-2). It does not matter whether a person is righteous or wicked, good or evil, all suffer the same situations in life. Moral distinctions count for nothing before indiscriminate death. William P. Brown thinks Koheleth's indictment against life on earth "offers nothing more than a tomb to die in."[3]

Everyone, regardless of merit or demerit will die. "This is an evil in all that happens under the sun, that the same fate comes to everyone" (9:3a). The Teacher thinks it is an "evil" that both good and bad people suffer the same experience of death. Michael Fox characterizes this as "equal fates for unequal people."[4]

The Teacher adds the moral dimension that all human beings are full of evil while they live. "Moreover, the hearts of all are full of evil; madness is in their hearts while they live, and after that they go to the dead" (9:3b). The problems of the fallen nature of human beings fit everyone. It characterizes the inner nature of a person (hearts). It lasts for a lifetime. Human beings share both a similar character (evil) and a similar fate (death).

Now readers want to close Ecclesiastes. They are tired of hearing about the toilsome task of living. But the Teacher refused to give in to total despair. He takes a turn to a more positive note. He concedes a hope among the living as he moves to his next thought.

Life's Superiority over Death

9:4-6

Even though the Teacher has described life full of evil and madness, he surprises his readers by indicating that life has hope. He asserts that life is better than death. He implies that there are advantages in being alive. "But whoever is joined with all the living has hope" (9:4a). Despite the numerous troubles in life, he thinks life is preferable to death. In life there is a time to enjoy the present and the future, but in death all possibility of future change of fortune is gone (vv. 5-6).[5]

The Teacher uses a proverb to support his assertion that life is better than death. "For a living dog is better than a dead lion" (9:4b). The lion and the dog furnish a graphic comparison. Western culture loves their dogs, but in the Old Testament dogs are portrayed as dirty, horrible animals. But the lion is a noble beast. It is the "king of the jungle." The lion's royal status is worthless in death. A dead lion is nothing more than a carcass fit for the vultures. The lion and the dog have conflicting reputations: intelligence and folly, might and weakness, majesty and lowliness. For Koheleth the groveling dog had an advantage over the dead lion. The point of the proverb is that life has a distinct advantage over death.

The Teacher presents another reason the living have superiority over the dead. "The living know that they will die, but the dead know nothing; they have no more reward, and even the memory of them is lost. Their love and their hate and their envy have already perished; never again will they have any share in all that happens under the sun" (9:5-6). The hope of the living begins with the awareness of death's certainty and points toward opportunities that avail themselves within the brief time span of life, especially those few and fleeting moments of joy. The living have self-awareness, but the dead do not. Furthermore, the dead have "no more reward." They have nothing to anticipate. Every the "memory of them is lost." Their past accomplishments are forgotten by those who live later.

The mention of love, hate, and envy (probably rivalry or striving for success in life) is not intended to be a catalog of all the qualities in the human character. Koheleth sees these rather as the strong passion which, admirable or not, forms the mainspring of human activities. Better to participate in these stimulating endeavors of life than to be dead with no passion and no activities at all.[6]

Perhaps no more pessimistic passage exists in Ecclesiastes than 9:5-6. It confronts readers with death. It does this without any clear indication of a life to come. Ecclesiastes tells about life "under the sun" or an earthly existence. This raises the questions: Is this life all there is? Is it possible that there could be an existence after one dies? Readers will have to wait for the New Testament for these questions to be answered.

Life's Possible Enjoyments

9:7-10

The Teacher changes his mood in 9:7-10. Previously in 9:2-6 he gives a dirge about death. But now he supplies an alternative possibility. Against the background of death, the Teacher gives some important advice for enjoying life in the present. The Teacher's attitude is encapsulated in an old Latin expression —*carpe diem*— "seize the day." In 9:7-10 he reached a greater level of intensity than in his previous enjoyment passages because the language is cast as a command. The imperative gives a sense of urgency to the possible enjoyment: go, eat, drink, let, enjoy, do. He urges readers to embrace the good life before it is too late. Seize the day before death seizes the self.

What enjoyments have been made possible by God for people to enjoy? The Teacher gives four activities in particular for the enjoyment of life. "Go, eat your bread with enjoyment, and drink your wine with a merry heart; for God has long ago approved what you do" (9:7). First, the Teacher urges readers to relish the simple pleasures of eating and drinking. These activities reflect the comforts of life. Nothing about discomfort is godly. The Teacher commands us to eat our bread and drink our wine with joyful heats. The real experience of food and drink is the enjoyment and merry heart commensurate with the activities.

The Teacher challenges life's expectations. We expect the swift to win the race, the strong to win the battle, the wise to be successful, the intelligent to be rich, and the skillful to be appreciated. But there are so many exceptions to our expectations. Why? Because "time and chance" occur to them all. Accidents happen: runners stumble; the smart can be outsmarted; the wise can lose their jobs; intelligent businesspeople can go broke; the skillful can lose favor. Koheleth emphasizes that humans cannot control life's happenings. Life is unpredictable.[7]

Second, Koheleth moves from enjoying the comforts of life to the celebration of life. "Let your garments always be white; do not let oil be lacking on your head" (9:8). The garments and the oil symbolize various kinds of celebration. White clothes were the dress clothes of the Near East. It would be comparable to the American tuxedo or the evening dress. Many people adorned white garments on special, festive occasions. The Teacher admonished his readers to waste no opportunity to seize whatever good things life has to offer. The Teacher also advises his listeners to pour oil on their head. The oil absorbed the heat and protected the skin from dryness. Some interpreters think that the oil also adds a good fragrance to the body. Harold Kushner tells than in the Talmud, the collected wisdom of the rabbis, there is a saying, "In the world to come, each of us will be called to account for all the good things God put on earth which we refused to enjoy."[8] The Teacher does not offer scorn for the body and its appetites. Instead, a sense of reverence exists for the pleasures of life, which God put here for our enjoyment, a way of seeing God in the world through the experience of pleasant moments.

Third, in addition to enjoying the comforts and the celebrations of life, the Teacher tells his readers to enjoy companionship. "Enjoy life with the wife whom you love, all the days of your vain life that are given you under the sun" (9:9a). The Teacher commends the daily pleasure of marriage and family life. Love and enjoyment go together. If you love your spouse, then be intentional about enjoying each other. When Koheleth mentioned the word "vain" in connection with companionship, he is not saying that companionship is meaningless but that it is short.

A fourth activity the Teacher recommends to make life enjoyable is work. "Because that is your portion in life and in your toil at which you toil under the sun. Whatever your hand finds to do, do with your might; for there is no work or thought or knowledge or wisdom in Sheol, to which you are going" (9:9b-10). The series of encouragements, comforts, celebrations, and companionship enable a person to put himself or herself into the tasks of life with energy and confidence.[9] To the Teacher work is a part of the joy of living. God created humans to work (Gen. 2:15). Purposeful work gives a person satisfaction and joy.

In view of the brevity of life and the certainty of death, the Teacher commands his readers to "seize the day." Eat your bread with enjoyment. Drink your wine with a merry heart. Enjoy life with the person you love. Now he commands, "Whatever your hand finds to do, do with all your might." He has turned the toil of work into a celebration in life. He has stripped the weariness from the work and transformed burdensome labor into a life-affirming vocation.[10]

Life ultimately comes to a close for all. Sheol is the place of the dead. Earth experiences, activities, plans, and wisdom cease. Sheol is characterized by the absence of opportunity for earthly life and its enjoyments. While we live and before death comes, the Teacher urges us to seize the day with various enjoyments.

Life's Inevitable Happenings

9:11-12

Koheleth has been talking about the enjoyment of the present in light of the reality of death. He now moves to a sobering reality, an honest appraisal. He talks about the unpredictability of our lives and the unexpectedness of our death. The present cannot be manipulated to our consistent enjoyment. Life's inevitable happenings in the present frustrate and disappoint the Teacher.

To stress the unpredictable happenings in ours lives, the Teacher gives a series of object lessons: the sprinter, the warrior, the wise man, and the skillful. "Again I saw that under the sun the race is not to the swift, nor the battle to the strong, nor bread to the wise, nor riches to the intelligent, nor favor to the skillful; but time and chance happen to them all" (9:11). Two factors seem to upset all human calculations. First, time limits humans. Second, chance is the unexpected event which may throw the most accomplished off course, despite the most thoroughly prepared plans and schemes.[11] Chance always has the upper hand rather than aspiration and preparation. "Next to death the only guarantee in life is that accidents will happen, and no one knows when and to whom they will strike."[12]

The issues surrounding chance, the unpredictability of life, are brought into explicit connection with death. No one knows when he is going to die. The Teacher illustrates the unexpectedness of death with two images from wildlife. "For no one can anticipate the time of disaster. Like fish taken in a cruel net, and like birds caught in a snare, so mortals are snared at a time of calamity, when it suddenly falls upon them" (9:12). Fish may swim casually along the stream, and birds may fly effortless though the air, but in a moment they may struggle in a trap that leads to the end of their lives. No amount of intellectual activity or moral discernment can deliver one from the snare of death.

Time and chance happen to all human beings. The word "time" could refer to the seasons of life. Before we know it, we become old or we become a victim of a bad situation. Of course when our time is over, the end of life occurs for us. Death is certain. It comes unexpectedly at times. While living on this earth, everyone needs to realize that bad things inevitably happen, and death inevitably comes.

Life's Great Resources

9:13-18

How does one live in the light of all these uncertainties. Some would think that the best way is to throw up your hand and resign to fate. The Teacher gives a different response. He commends the relative value of earthly wisdom. He tells how to live each day—value wisdom. He teaches by giving an example of someone who acted wisely. "I have also seen this example of wisdom under the sun, and it seemed great to me. There was a little city with few people in it. A great king came against it and besieged it, building great siegeworks against it. Now there was found in it a poor wise man, and he by his wisdom delivered the city. Yet no one remembered that poor man" (9:13-15). The Teacher observed a situation that made a great impact on him. He was struck by the struggle of prestige (a great king) and insignificance (a poor wise man). He sees a small city being besieged by a powerful king. From the perspective of manpower and resources, the city did not stand a chance.

But the city was rescued by a surprising source, a poor wise man. The Teacher does not specify what the wise man did to save the city. He merely says the poor man by his wisdom saved the city. The story illustrates wisdom's ability and benefits.

The Teacher closes the story by telling how the city's inhabitants completely forgot what the poor wise man did. People are fickle, and fame is fleeting. In a culture of confusion, wisdom leaves scarcely a trace. The wise person remains unnoticed in a city beset by folly. Wisdom has a hard time surviving in the best of all possible worlds.[13]

Koheleth applies the lesson of the example, namely, that wisdom is not often heeded or remembered. The Teacher assesses the value of wisdom of the living of our days. "So I said, 'Wisdom is better than might; yet the poor man's wisdom is despised, and his words are not heeded. The quiet words of the wise are more to be heeded than the shouting of a ruler among fools. Wisdom is better than weapons of war, but one bugle destroys much good" (9:16-18). The Teacher loved to show the value of something by claiming one thing was better than another. He uses two "better than" proverbs to conclude the section. He promoted wisdom over folly and physical powers.

Koheleth's first "better than" proverb praises the quiet

words of wisdom over the loud words of fools. He contrasts the speech of the two with "quiet word" and "shouting." The wise person lets the wisdom of what he says speak for itself. Quiet words of wisdom have a lot more value than shouting foolish words.

The positive assessment of wisdom continues with a second "better than" proverb. The Teacher evaluates wisdom as superior to weapons of war. He notes that it takes little to destroy something good. One bugler can destroy much good. Wisdom is powerful and beneficial, but it may be rendered powerless by a minor indiscretion.

The Teacher seems to have become a specialist on life by means of his keen observation and his inward soundings. He looked closely, honestly, wisely, and he learned a lot. He pondered what he saw. Fortunately, he passed his observation on to a needy world. He saw that all human beings go through the same kind of experiences. He loves life and its activities, and he laments that life has to end. He praises life as being superior to death. He did not linger too long looking at the reality of death. Instead, he moved to share some possible moments life affords before it is over. But he has to be a realist. Life has many unpredictable trials and an unexpected death. To cope with time and chance, Koheleth recommends wisdom. It is the forgotten virtue.

Chapter 12

A Scrutiny of Foolish People

10:1-20

Sinclair Ferguson in his book The Pundit's Folly tells of an interesting sight. Outside the town of Oban on the west coast of Scotland stands an interesting building. It overlooks the bay at Oban on Battery Hill. When the building is seen from a distance, it looks like the Roman Coliseum.

As sightseers get closer to the building, they are shocked to see a mere shell. Actually, the construction consists of nothing more than a circular wall. It has many windows, and it is amazingly symmetrical. It was built by John Stuart McCaig between 1897 and 1902. It cost more than five hundred British pounds. McCaig build the wall to provide a lasting monument to his family and to provide work for the stonemasons during the off-season of the winter months. The edifice, now more than a century old, is named after its builder McCaig's Folly.

In architecture a "folly" is a building constructed primarily for decoration. Many such buildings litter the British countryside. Some can be seen in France. These buildings date from the eighteenth to the nineteenth centuries. They have been constructed to impress, but they serve no other function. They are useless and empty facades. They are "follies," and people consider the wealthy builders foolish.[1]

Koheleth did not look at buildings, but he did observe foolish people. In 10:1–20 the words "fool," "folly," and "foolishness" appear frequently. The term "folly" (*sekel*) or "fool" (*sakal*) is associated with wickedness, and it is the opposite of wisdom (2:19). It comes from an inner deficiency of the heart, which becomes obvious to observers, especially in the fool's speech and action. Koheleth see the foolish ones "skilled in doing evil" (cf. Jer. 4:22).

     Ecclesiastes 10 does not appear to be carefully and logically written. It contains case studies, short stories, maxims, proverbs, comparisons, and exhortations. But throughout the chapter the words "folly" or "fool" seem to unify the chapter. The Teacher makes a careful scrutiny of what foolish people think, say, or do. He makes a clear contrast between two ways to live, the wise way and the foolish way.[2]

     Before working through chapter 10, we need to understand more about the meaning of *sakal* or "fool" and *sekel* or "folly." Neither term describes a person with inferior intelligence. The word *sakal* or "fool" is peculiar to Koheleth and never occurs in Proverbs. The term seems to describe people who lacked the proper fear of God, and they are prone to speak and to act in opposition to God. "Fool say in their hearts, 'There is no God'" (Ps. 14:1). The entire chapter of Ecclesiastes 10 focuses on folly. Koheleth sees people making wrong choices, lacking in discernment and discretion, and speaking foolishly. He gives scrutiny to people living life in a senseless manner.

Foolish Action

10:1-4

Koheleth begins with the sight of foolish actions people commit. The first four verses of chapter 10 contain a cluster of proverbs which takes folly or foolishness as the theme. The Teacher makes a point with a proverb: "Dead flies make the perfumer's ointment give off a foul odor; so a little folly outweighs wisdom and honor" (10:1). A small rotting fly in a batch of perfume ruins the sweet smell of valuable perfume. The Teacher's point is that a little of a bad thing like folly spoils much of a good thing like wisdom.[3] Nobert Lohfink contends that the Hebrew word translated "folly" could mean "stupid." Up to this point "folly" was considered a lack of education. It was something that could be remedied. It was not stupidity. The word seems to be used as the unwise use of a person's intellect.[4]

As stench is the antithesis of a sweet fragrance, so is "heart of the wise" the opposite of "heart of the fool." "The heart of the wise inclines to the right, but the heart of a fool to the left" (10:2). The "heart of the wise" describes the seat of intelligence and the will. The opposite direction of right and left do not refer to theological or political leanings but to moral actions. The right refers to good and favor in biblical tradition, and the left refers to what is wrong or inferior. Folly distinguishes itself from wisdom.

Koheleth now uses a picture to talk about the principle of folly. "Even when fools walk on the road, they lack sense, and show to everyone that they are fools" (10:3). There is nothing subtle or hidden about folly. It inevitably showcases itself. The Teacher gives a picture of a fool walking on a road. He does not specify exactly what the fool does, but he makes the point clearly that when people see him they will know that he is a fool.

Koheleth makes clear that the way the heart is leaning determines one's behavior. The fool does not know he is acting senselessly. Foolish people take the wrong road in life, and they cannot even find their way to town on a clearly marked road. The Teacher pushes home the point that the way of wisdom is better than folly.

Foolish Leadership

10:4-7

The next proverbial cluster focuses on political leadership. The Teacher set the state with an image of a foolish ruler who loses his temper. "If the anger of the ruler rises against you, do not leave your post, for calmness will undo great offenses" (10:4). The Teacher advises employees of the royal court to maintain a calm composure when subjected to the king's wrath. Anger needs not to be met with revenge or fear but with a placating calmness, for only by such a response is their hope of resolution. Anger met by anger brings needless conflict and destruction. The writer of Proverbs wrote, "A soft anger turns away wrath, but a harsh word stirs up anger" (15:1).

Koheleth turns to another group of proverbs that describe power in various areas of leadership. "There is an evil that I have seen under the sun, as great an error as if it proceeded from the ruler: folly is set in many high places, and the rich sit in a low place. I have seen slaves on horseback, and princes walking on foot like slaves" (10:5-7). The Teacher points out that in some cases the wrong people have been promoted to leadership. Uneducated slaves receive powerful positions that they cannot handle in a wise manner. Other people, who have the advantages of good training or wise leadership, get left in humble and obscure positions. Koheleth thinks this is political foolishness. He attributes "evil" to someone who holds the reins of leadership power and has upset the status quo. The fool and the wise have traded places. In the area of leadership, the benefits of wisdom are easily lost to a foolish reversal of appointment. The Teacher pictures an unhappy condition when incompetent people are in authority and they lord over the ones who really should be in charge.

Foolish Thinking

10:8-11

The next cluster of proverbs offers insights related to work. Failing to think or to keep your mind on your work could lead to risks. The expression in 10:11 "wisdom helps one to succeed" provides the key for understanding this group of proverbs. One must use wisdom in work activities such as digging a pit, remodeling a house, working with heavy stone, or splitting logs. To perform such activities carelessly or foolishly risks great danger. Likewise, it is a foolish snake charmer who uses his charming techniques after getting bitten.

"Whoever digs a pit will fall into it; and whoever breaks through a wall will be bitten by a snake. Whoever quarries stones will be hurt by them; and whoever splits logs will be endangered by them. If the iron is blunt, and one does not whet the edge, then more strength must be exerted; but wisdom helps one to succeed. If the snake bites before it is charmed, there is no advantage in the charmer" (10:8–11). Possibly the "pit" refers to a trap for animals. It was camouflaged. If the person who dug the pit did not pay careful attention to the pit he dug, he would easily fall into the pit. A stone fence, which consists of unhewn stone joined without mortar, could provide a nest for poisonous snakes. Workers who quarry stones or split logs can easily be injured. Koheleth presents examples of hazardous occupations in which a little bit of wisdom can help minimize the risk.

Wisdom makes good sense. Thinking people will sharpen the axe. It helps them lessen the energy of the task at hand. Cutting through wood with a dull axe is a difficult task. Wisdom helps one know to sharpen the axe.

The Teacher continues with commonsense thinking with the strange illustration of charming a snake. If the snake bites before it is charmed, the charmer will get bitten. But if he uses wisdom, he will make sure the snake is charmed before he handles it. Since a little folly can get us in deep trouble, we need to use wisdom in our daily work.

Foolish Words

10:12-14

Koheleth kept looking at life. Not only did he see the actions of fools, but he also heard their words. Sooner or later all wisdom writings deal with words. The nature of one's conversation is the crucial test of wisdom. In 10:12-14 the Teacher mentions self-edifying words as conveyed by the wise and self-destructive words spoken by fools. People's words indicate whether they are wise or foolish.

The speech of the fool is compared to that of the wise. "Words spoken by the wise bring them favor, but the lips of fools consume them" (10:12). Words of the wise bring favor, but the words of fools bring harm. Fools get caught in their own words. Many people get in trouble with their words.

The fool's words may be traced to the inner character of a person. "The words of their mouth begin in foolishness, and their talk ends in wicked madness" (10:13). Conversation comes from character. At first the fool's conversation is mere foolishness, but the words progress to "wicked madness." The fool's words degenerate into immorality.

The fool also talks incessantly about subjects he or she knows nothing about. "Yet fools talk on and on. No one knows what is to happen, and who can tell anyone what the future holds?"(10:14). Fools are opinionated. They tend to be big talkers. The fools are so foolish that they do keep their folly to themselves. They insist on sharing it with others. Fools talk on and on, even when they do not know what they are talking about.

Foolish people like to talk about the future. They think they know what the future holds. The Teacher reminds us that no one really knows the future and what is going to happen. What makes people fools is they think they can talk about the future with certainty. Their words show their senselessness.

Foolish Incompetency

10:15-20

The Teacher continues to report his careful scrutiny of foolish people. He sees them to be highly incompetent. Not only are the actions and words of fools senseless, but they cannot successfully accomplish the simplest tasks. "The toil of fools wears them out, for they do not even know the way to town" (10:15). Not being able to find their way home reflects a gross incompetency. Ancient cities were built on hilltops or mounds, and they were conspicuous. Fools do not have the most elementary thinking. This saying in verse 15 seems to communicate a stupidity comparable to the common saying, "He does not know enough to come in out of the rain."[5]

The Teacher returns to the political arena and contrasts two opposite political orders. The first political order is the upside-down order where the fool reigns. "Alas for you, O land, when your king is a servant, and your princes feast in the morning!" (10:16). A dirge is directed to a land ruled by an immature ruler. It is not good for the land when the king is a servant or a child. The word "servant" is a term designating youth and/or subservience.

The incompetency of the king shows up on the incompetency of the princes, the secondary leaders. Feasting in the morning marked a dissolute, slothful approach to leadership. Emphasis was on luxury and personal indulgence.

The second political order is the organized reign of the wise leader. "Happy are you, O land, when your king is a nobleman, and your princes feast at the proper time—for strength, and not for drunkenness" (10:17). The emphasis is not so much on age. It is a comparison between a mature and an immature approach to leadership. Another criterion for competency may be seen in the self-control of the secondary leaders, the princes. The enjoyment of life's pleasures makes national happiness. But the pseudo-enjoyment of self-centered indulgence is a mark of national disaster.

Incompetent leaders lead to deterioration in a nation. The nation with a foolish political order is like a house that is not maintained. "Through sloth the roof sinks in, and through indolence the house leaks" (10:18). The king is incompetent and the princes are off feasting. Koheleth, in verse 18, seems to state the perspective of the princes. "Feasts are made for laughter; wine gladdens life, and money meets every need" (10:19). The princes are focused merely on the good times not the responsibility of running the affairs of government. They have their parties, their wine, and a public expense account. Let the good times roll!

Meanwhile, no one has looked out for the land while the good times take place. The people suffered. They were tempted to curse the king, but the Teacher warns against it. "Do not curse the king, even in your thoughts, or curse the rich, even in your bedroom; for a bird of the air may carry your voice, or some winged creature tell the matter"(10:20). The danger of cursing the king is too great. People need to be careful how they speak about those in authority, for words have a way of reaching others. The Teacher warns not to speak evil of the king, even in the secret recesses of the mind. He then advises against cursing the rich, who are powerful, in the secret recesses of that house. Perhaps Koheleth's warning is the origin of the expression, "A little bird told me."

The Teacher has given close attention to the fool. He sees the fool's way of thinking by the way the fool acts and speaks. He has seen the fool's actions, the fool's leadership, the fool's thinking, the fool's words, and the fool's incompetency. No one need be a fool. God's will can rescue anyone from folly. God's wisdom will help keep people from living the life of foolishness.

Chapter 13

A Glimpse at a Better Life

11:1-10

The writer of Ecclesiastes cannot be accused of being blind to the realities of life. He has not neglected us as he introduced us to reality. His discourses in Ecclesiastes 1–10 contain careful examinations of the negative side of life. Ecclesiastes begins on a negative note in 1:2 with the mention on the word "vanity." That word continues to appear for thirty-eight times as the writer looked at creation, the law courts, the marketplace, human relationships, the house of God, disappointed people, and the mania for money. Each time the writer observed a particular situation, he assessed it in a negative manner—vanity. He even added that numerous pursuits in life produced nothing more than a chasing of the wind. He became rather fatalistic at one point saying there was nothing to be gained under the sun.

Some readers of Ecclesiastes have assed the original author as a nihilist. These interpreters think the writer believed that all of life is senseless and there is no possibility of an objective basis for truth. Closer reading of Ecclesiastes denies that the writer was a nihilist. He was negative at times. He was realistic though, and this realism caused him to be interpreted as negative more times than he really was. Early in the book he allowed for the possibility that life may be enjoyed in the present. He stressed the pursuit of the simple pleasures of life. If there is no ultimate meaning in wisdom, in one's work, in pleasures, in success, or in wealth, then one must look to enjoy life as the opportunities present themselves. Throughout Ecclesiastes the writer has six times urged readers to seize the temporal pleasures that light the burden of life (2:24–26; 3:12–14, 22; 5:18–20; 8:15; 9:7–10). So, you see, the writer of Ecclesiastes did not give up on life. He did not capitulate to cynicism or allow despair to take over his thinking.

Koheleth moves away from observations that lead to negative assessments. He articulates what he has seen throughout Ecclesiastes, and that is the possibility of a better life. Depression and despair do not have to be the only responses to life. The Teacher goes in the direction of advice or suggestions for a better life. In Ecclesiastes 11 the Teacher gives advice rather than makes observations. He assumes the role of a therapist rather than a mere reporter. He gives five recommendations for a better life: seize opportunities (1–2), master moments (3–5), accept mysteries (6), enjoy life (7-8), and choose happiness (9-10).

Seize Opportunities

11:1-2

Koheleth begins with a curious piece of advice. "Send out your bread upon the waters, for after many days you will get it back" (11:1). This is a famous and oft-quoted verse. Unfortunately some interpreters read meaning into this verse that probably was not intended by the writer. What did the Teacher have in mind when he suggests sending bread out on the waters? Obviously he was not speaking literally of putting bread on the water. Two reasonable interpretations have been proposed for verse 1. Both interpretations could result in the same application. The thrust of the verse with either interpretation seems to be "seize opportunities."

Many commentators think the Teacher referred to the sea trade.[1] The allusion is to the element of trust in much ancient business on the sea. Sea trading involved a risky business. The journeys were long and dangerous. Owners who put their cargo on ships could not trace the ship's course. They had no idea how the vessels fared. In the Kings material we learn that Solomon had a fleet of ships that would return with gold, silver, and ivory once every three years (1 Kings 10:22). With the shipping industry in mind, the Teacher encourages owners to ship their grain across the sea, and after many days the ships could return with other cargo. Therefore, the latter part of verse one "for after many days you will get it back" could refer to the ship's return. The owner must dare to take a risk if he wants a return. In a similar manner the Teacher calls his readers to take life as a gift from the hand of God and to exercise trust and adventure. Seize opportunities.

Other commentators think the Teacher suggests works of charity.[2] This interpretation seems to be more in line with Near Eastern parallels, as well as with the history of interpretation. Compare Ecclesiastes 11:1 with an Arabic proverb: "Do good, throw your bread on the waters, and one day you will find it."[3] Koheleth probably refers to the good deed given freely. The proverb contends that in the act of giving, something is inevitably given back. What is given does not dissipate or vanish.

William P. Brown gives an excellent illustration to explain this interpretation. He relates how in Barbara Kingsolver's novel Animal Dreams, a young horticulturist named Hallie has gone to Nicaragua to aid the peasants. In a letter to her sister Codi back in the states, she explains her reasons: "Wars and elections are both too big and too small to matter in the long run. The daily work—that goes on, it adds up. It goes into the ground, into crops, into children's bellies, and their bright eyes. Good things don't get lost."[4] "Good things don't get lost" is precisely Koheleth's point.

Interpreters of verse 1 who think the Teacher is writing about works of philanthropy think that sometime in the future you will reap a reward. Of course this is not the suggestion to be generous so that the giver may reap a reward. True integrity in giving does not look for a reward when helping others. In Charles Dickens's *The Christmas Carol*, Mr. Scrooge changes from a squeezing, wrenching, grasping, scraping, clutching, covetous sinner onto a man whose "heart laughed." The change came when he sent his bread on the water and gave a portion to seven, or even to eight, both of which mean many people.[5]

Koheleth continues with his suggestion to seize opportunities. "Divide your means seven ways, or even eight, for you do not know what disaster may happen on earth" (11:2). If the Teacher meant sending ships on a business venture, his suggestions in verse 2 would mean to spread the risk. Do not put all of your opportunities on one ship. If the Teacher meant generous giving, his suggestion would mean to share your charitable gifts with a larger community.

The Teacher's advice, whatever the specific interpretation, is to seize opportunities in life. The businessperson must seize opportunities in seafaring. If he does not send out ships, the ships will not return with profitable cargo. Owners will never make money unless they venture to ship their cargo. People who have gifts will never help others if they do not seize the opportunities to give. Only when they take advantage of opportunities do they have the possibility of bringing profit to themselves or to enrich the lives of others. The Teacher suggests for his readers to seize opportunities, and then he moves to another suggestion for a better life.

Master Moments

11:3-4, 6

Koheleth closed his previous section with "for you do not know what disaster may happen on earth." The Teacher proceeds to expand on that line. He points to some of the regularities, the certainties one can observe in nature. "When clouds are full, they empty rain on the earth" (11:3a). Heavy clouds in Palestine send a meaningful signal. Residents knew it was going to rain. We observe this phenomenon of nature all the time. Heavy clouds indicate the possibility of rain.

The Teacher gives another example of nature's certainties. "Whether a tree falls to the south or to the north, in the place where the tree falls, there it will lie" (11:3b). A tree falls to the ground. It could fall to the north or to the south, to the east or to the west. Sidney Greidanus thinks the point of the example is that where the tree falls, it will lie. A fallen tree is not going to move in a different direction from where it fell. This happens all the time. It is a law of nature.[6] These illustrations of the cloud and the tree speak to human inability to control life. No one can determine when the clouds will produce rain. And no one can control where a tree will fall.

The Teacher transitions from nature's certainties to mastering the appropriate moment for farming. Obsessive weather watching will not guarantee a productive yield. Farmers who try to control their circumstances will never get anywhere. Agriculture carries with it the necessity of mastering appropriate moments. "Whoever observes the wind will not sow; and whoever regards the clouds will not reap" (11:4). Humans cannot control the wind or the rain. Farmers who wait for perfect weather conditions will never get a harvest because they are afraid to plant for fear the seed will be blown away. They will also be afraid to harvest for fear the rain will come before the crops are gathered.[7] This illustration of the farmer teaches us that a lot of life is beyond our control, and we need to take advantage of the joys and privileges of each day.

In 11:6 the Teacher urges the farmer to master the appropriate moment and to work boldly and wisely. "In the morning sow your seed, and at evening do not let your hands be idle; for you do not know which will prosper, this or that, or whether both alike will be good" (11:6). Some people do not take the appropriate moment to sow, and therefore they will not reap. Others wait too long, and they waste a harvest. Sow your seed in the morning and in the evening. No one knows whether the evening of the morning will be the best time for sowing, so the best action is to sow in the morning and in the evening. Seize the proper moment.

Waiting until we are absolutely sure what God wants us to do and when he wants us to do it means waiting for a long time. This is no excuse for sitting around and doing nothing. Do not act like that farmer waiting for the wind to change. Master the moment and sow your seed. Nothing brings greater sadness than looking back and seeing numerous missed opportunities. This leads to the "if onlys." Do what you have to do; do what you can do, and do it now.[8]

The suggestion for a better life is neither acting too soon or too late. It is to act at just the right moment.

Accept Limitations

11:5

The Teacher does not always follow a sequential pattern in his teachings. He often mentions one truth and then proceeds to another and another then goes back to a former or first truth. The Teacher seems to advise readers to accept their human limitations. Four times in six verses the Teacher says "you do not know": "you do not know that disaster may happen on earth" (11:2b), "you do not know how the breath comes to the bones in the mother's womb" (11:5a), "you do not know the work of God" (11:5b), and "you do not know which will prosper" (11:6b). Throughout Ecclesiastes the Teacher insists that humans must recognize that God is infinite and humans are finite. With his words "you do not know," Koheleth was not speaking negatively of the human race. Instead, he was speaking realistically about human limitations.

Human beings can never understand all of the issues in life. "Just as you do not know how the breath comes to the bones in the mother's womb, so you do not know the work of God, who makes everything" (11:5). Probably the meaning of "wind" in verse 4 continues into verse 5. Just as humans do not know the way of the wind, so they do not know how breath comes in the womb to the child. The words "wind" and "breath" come from the same Hebrew word (ruah). Koheleth teaches that there are some experiences in life we do not know, namely the mystery of the wind and the mystery of conception and birth.

The Teacher goes on to add that there are certain aspects of God working on earth that defy explanation. God's work in creation cannot be explained fully. In 2004 the Hubble Space Telescope photographed a tiny sliver of space through prolonged exposures that lasted for more than eleven days. Then astronomers counted the number of galaxies in the photograph. In that tiny sliver of the universe they found ten thousand galaxies, each containing one hundred billion stars.[9]

Scientists are also trying to discover tangible evidence for the last atomic particle, the Higgs boson. Probably when they observe it—if they ever do—they will wonder if there is something even smaller. Truly God "does great things and unsearchable, marvelous things without number" (Job 5:9). The whole universe contains mysteries from inside the atom to the most distant star in space.[10]

What God does among the created order is a great mystery. But what God does in human lives is also mysterious. No one can fully know God's ways. We can feel the effect of the wind and see the results of fetal development. We can see God working in the world. But how he is working and why he is working lie beyond our human comprehension. The truths in verse 5 drive the readers to a sense of being human. The life of faith does not remove the problem of human ignorance. It enables us to live with it. Faith flourishes in the mystery of providence.[11]

Trying to be omnipotent or omniscient leads to a frustrating life. Humans cannot be God. They must be satisfied in being human. Koheleth's word to accept limitations leads to a better, more enjoyable life.

Enjoy Life

11:7-9

The Teacher has been reminding his readers that there is much we do not know. We have many questions to which we have no answers. One thing, however, we do know. Life itself is sweet and pleasant, and we ought to be grateful for each day of life and enjoy it. The Teacher strongly recommends people to enjoy life on earth. He comes with a surprising statement: "Light is sweet, and it is pleasant for the eyes to see the sun" (11:7). These are not the words of a full-blown pessimist. These words come from a realist who encourages the enjoyment of life.

Koheleth portrays the goodness of life with light. Elsewhere in the Old Testament light is used to connote joy and blessing in contrast to the darkness of adversity and death. It means to be "joyfully alive." "To see the sun" means not merely to live and exist but to live joyfully, enthusiastically. It is good for a person to see the sun each day, or to say it another way, "It is good to be alive."

Koheleth does not just describe the goodness of life; he encourages us to enjoy life's goodness. "Even those who live many years should rejoice in them all; yet let them remember that the days of darkness will be many. All that comes is vanity" (11:8). Enjoyment of life needs to be a lifelong experience. Sometimes we neglect the present by looking too much in the past or thinking too much about the future. Koheleth wants his students to live a day at a time and not to waste a day. He continues his realism by reminding his readers that dark days, the days of suffering and bereavement, will inevitably come. Even though dark days come, we can enjoy the days of light.

This sort of realism debunks many of the ways people commonly think they can enjoy life. Alcohol, drugs, unrestrained sex, abundant entertainment, and other pleasures seem to bring enjoyment. Perhaps, briefly, they do bring a degree of enjoyment for the short term. But the dark days come, and these pursuits seem to be of little value. Koheleth urges us to grab the sweetness of life as long as it lasts, for death will inevitably come with all the empty meaninglessness that it brings with it.

The Teacher urges the young to enjoy the days of youth. "Rejoice, young man, while you are young, and let your heart cheer you in the days of your youth. Follow the inclinations of your heart and the desire of your eyes, but know that for all these things God will bring you into judgment" (11:9). The word "rejoice" means to make the most of your youth. Enjoy it. The command "follow" invites living in the ways of your heart and in the sight of your eyes. He does not invite youth to gratify every passion or to follow the lead of the roving eye. The term "heart" is the mind that ensures self-control. The "desire of your eyes" is that assessment of life you would expect a person of wisdom to have.[12]

We must not misunderstand the Teacher's final comment in verse 9 that "for all these things God will bring you into judgment." More that likely the Teacher is not thinking of any final judgment beyond this present life. He seems to be thinking about what we do with hour lives here and now. That seems to be what matters to God. He will hold us responsible for the way we handle his gifts to us.[13]

Don't judge a book until you have read all of the chapters. The tone may change. Many people become depressed reading about the vanity, absurdity, meaninglessness, and pointlessness assessed to life in the early chapters of Ecclesiastes. Thankfully, you have stayed with the study of Ecclesiastes until chapter 11. It gives pictures of a better life! It even tells us to enjoy life!

Choose Joy

11:10

The Teacher moves to a final suggestion about how to have a better life. In this suggestion he admonishes his students to live a joyful life. "Banish anxiety from your mind, and put away pain from your body; for youth and the dawn of life are vanity" (11:10). Certain problems that beset both mind and body threaten the life of joy. The choice of joy is emphasized with two verbs associated with removal: "banish" and "put away." Youth goes away; life is a vapor. It is here one minute and gone the next. Therefore, while young "banish anxiety from your mind." The Hebrew word for "anxiety" refers to that which angers, grieves, or irritates. Koheleth urged the removal of anxiety from the mind.

The second problem that hinders joy is that which besets our bodies. The Hebrew word for "pain" portrays humanity in their weaknesses, both physical weariness and moral frailty. If bodily pain or discomfort can be removed, it should be. So, while you are young, you should, as much as possible, get rid of pain and suffering. Put away anxiety from your mind and pain from your body.

Koheleth emphasizes that childhood and youth pass quickly. These years are precious and need to be treated responsibly. The Hebrew word for "youth" can mean the blackening of hair as opposed to the gray hair of age. Youth is also the time of "dawning." It is the beginning. Before one knows it, the sun will start to set. Therefore, the Teacher urges one to make the most of the "dawning years."

Koheleth's call to choose joy is an urgent one for both young and old alike. The Teacher's call rests in the fundamental assumption that life is vanity—a vapor that appears for a while and then is gone. Shakespeare's song in Twelfth Night has a line: "Youth's a stuff will not endure."[14] Koheleth challenges his students to live in the present to the fullest.

The Teacher has looked at life honestly and comprehensively. He has seen the good and the bad. At times he dwelt excessively on the bad causing his students to think for a while that life is not worthwhile. It is meaningless. Thankfully, the Teacher continued to look. As he looked at life, he began to think within himself. The results of his inner processing come forward in the latter part of his work on Ecclesiastes. The book is closing on a more optimistic note that there is the possibility of a better life.

Chapter 14

A Command to Remember the Creator

12:1-14

Frederick Buechner tells of a dream he had in his book *A Room Called Remember*. He dreamed that he was staying in a hotel somewhere, and he loved the room the clerk gave him. The room, according to Buechner, gave him pleasant feelings. He felt happy and at peace in that room. Everything was to him as it should be and everything about himself seemed the way it should be too. As his dream progressed, he wandered to other places, but he always came back from his travels to the same hotel.

One time when he came back to the hotel, he was given a different room. He did not feel comfortable in it at all. The room felt dark and cramped. He made his way down to the man at the desk and told him that he had a problem with his room. He told about an earlier visit where he had this marvelous room. If possible, he would like the room again. (Remember, all of this takes place in a dream.) He did not know exactly where the room was. The clerk understood.

He said that he knew the room where he had stayed. He could have it next time and future times just by asking for the room by name. Beuchner in his dream asked for the name of the room. The clerk said, "The name of the room is Remember."[1]

The word remember appears frequently throughout the Bible. The Lord said, "Remember the sabbath day, and keep it holy" (Exod. 20:8). Israel had not intellectually forgotten the Sabbath. They had just let other days become more important than the day of rest and worship. The call to remember the Sabbath means to put the Sabbath day in the preeminent place in their lives. In one of Moses' speeches recorded in Deuteronomy, he warned Israel not to forget to keep the commands of God. How could these people forget intellectually the miracle of deliverance across the sea. Moses wanted the people to keep prominently and foremost in their minds how God had delivered them from Egypt.

In an upper room during the last week of his life, Jesus gave the disciples bread and wine and said, "Do this in remembrance of me" (Luke 22:19). The Lord knew the disciples would not forget intellectually his work on the cross. But they would let other issues and activities become more important than Christ. Therefore, he gave a way to remember him, to put him back in the preeminent place of their lives.

Koheleth invites his readers to stay in "the room called Remember." "Remember your creator in the days of your youth" (12:1a). The Teacher writes Ecclesiastes at a crucial time in Israel's history. The nation experienced the economic boom of international trade. People focused on money and the storing of wealth. They gave themselves to searching for satisfaction in endless entertainment and plentiful pleasures. They had arrived at a place in their lives where they lived day and night in the dark rooms of economic emptiness, vocational boredom, illicit sex, futile education, and many other dark rooms. Koheleth calls Israel to put God back in the foremost part of their hearts and minds. God wants to shape their view of life and handle the enigmas of their lives. The Teacher calls Israel to remember.

The dominant word in Koheleth's message recording in chapter 12 is "remember." The Teacher does not say, "Remember God." Instead, he says, "Remember your creator." The Creator is to the One who made us and gave us life. The Creator made our family and friends as well as every other human being. Our Creator made this marvelous world for us to live in and to manage. To remember means more than to recall intellectually that there is a Creator. It means to put the Creator prominently in your thinking and to focus your life on doing his will. Thoughout Ecclesiastes 12 Koheleth hammers home the call to dwell in the room called "Remember."

An Honest Look at Life: Ecclesiastes

The Urgency of Remembrance

12:1-8

Koheleth speaks of an urgency for remembering your Creator. He says, "Remember your creator in the days of your youth, before the days of trouble come, and the years draw near when you will say, 'I have no pleasure in them'" (12:1). The days of youth traditionally can be times to be carefree when the serious things of life can be postponed. But life is brief even at its longest. If opportunities are not seized during the days of youth, they could be missed. If godly habits are not adopted during the days of youth, a future time may be too late. To drive home the urgency of remembering, the Teacher writes about the experience of old age and death.[2]

The Teacher drives home the point that we have to remember the Creator before it is too late. Notice the three usages of the word "before"—"Remember your creator in the days of your youth, before the days of trouble come" (12:1a). "Before the sun and the night and the moon and the stars are darkened" (12:2a). "Before the silver cord is snapped" (12:6).

An incentive to act during your youth is the coming of old age. Increasing years bring inevitable decline, affecting one's whole life. The latter years often force one to be dependent on others once more. Koheleth says the older person declares, "I have no pleasure in them" (12:1b).

The activities of old age change from those of youth. "Before the sun and the light and the moon and the stars are darkened, and the clouds return with the rain" (12:2). The Teacher likens growing old and the approaching of death to an oncoming storm. The sun, moon, and stars are symbols of joy, but during old age they recede into the background while the storms (clouds) take center stage.

Body functions decline in old age. "In the days when the guards of the house tremble, and the strong men are bent, and the women who grind cease working because they are few, and those who look through the windows see dimly" (12:3). Koheleth pictures old age as a deteriorating house. The deteriorating house reminds the Teacher that humans grow weaker and weaker until they die. The Teacher gives poetic pictures of advancing age. The "guards of the house" could refer to the legs. They are no longer strong. The arms tremble. Men and women alike can no longer work because of the deterioration of strength. The expression "those who look through the windows see dimly" depict failing eyesight.

Advanced years create limited activity. "When the doors on the street are shut, and the sound of grinding is low, and one rises up at the sound of a bird, and all the daughters of song are brought low" (12:4). As years progress, people become shut-ins; that is, the doors of the street are closed. They cannot get out of the house. Old age prevents people from working; the grinding is low. Increasing age also causes insomnia, and one can be awakened even with the sound of a bird. The hearing leaves also, thus the daughter's song cannot be heard. Koheleth is deeply troubled by the idea of aging.

Koheleth continues with the poetic pictures of the aging process. "When one is afraid of heights, and terrors are on the road; the almond tree blossoms, the grasshopper drags itself along and desire fails; because all must go to their eternal home, and the mourners will go about the streets" (12:5). The Teacher mentioned four different characteristics of aging. The first is fear of heights and journey. The second is suggested by the silver blossom of the almond tree, or silver hair. The third is the difficulty of walking. And the fourth is the decline of sexual desire. The coming of old age calls everyone in their youth to remember their Creator.

Koheleth gives another urgent reason to remember the Creator in the days of youth. It is the coming of death. It may come after a long life, or it could come unexpectedly during youth. The Teacher pictures death in four expressions, which divide into two pairs. "Before the silver cord is snapped, and the golden bowl is broken, and the pitcher is broken at the fountain, and the wheel broken at the cistern, and the dust returns to the earth as it was, and the breath returns to God who gave it" (12:6–7). The first two pairs pictures a golden bowl and a wheel used to draw water from a cistern. The bowl falls, breaks, and is irreparably damaged. The second image portrays a wheel broken and the pitchers crash into the cistern. Both pictures point to the end of life where usefulness is over.

The next two pairs involve the return to dust and the return of the spirit to God. Returning to dust pictures the death of an individual and the decay of the body. The departing spirit means there no longer remains breath or life to animate the human body.

Readers can notice a change from 12:7 to 12:8. Koheleth's speeches cease in 12:8. A change from the first person to the third person appears in 12:8–14 ("says the Teacher'). Someone is speaking about Koheleth in the last verses of the book. As stated in chapter 1 of this work, this is the unnamed wisdom Teacher who is now using Koheleth's various observations as instruction to his son ("my child" 12:12a). The narrator begins with a summary of Koheleth's teaching. "Vanity of vanities, says the Teacher; all is vanity" (12:8). The narrator cites this typical phrase in order to give what he considers to be Koheleth's bottom line. Though Koheleth offered glimmers of home here and there in his observations, he seemed to think of life as meaningless. Oddly enough, the narrator began his introduction to the Teacher's speech in 1:2 and concluded the Teacher's speech in 12:8. Thus 1:2 and 12:8 form a kind of frame around the body of Ecclesiastes. In verses 9–12 the narrator will continue with his evaluation of Koheleth.

Descriptions of Remembrance

12:9–12

After summarizing Koheleth's teaching, the narrator begins his evaluation of the Teacher's communication techniques as well as more summarizations of his message. He starts with a description of Koheleth's work that is somewhat complimentary of Koheleth's teaching. The narrator wanted readers to understand more about the command to "remember your creator." The call to remember has nothing to do with the resurgence of intellectual forgetfulness. It has to do with making our Creator the foundation of our lives and the One foremost in our thoughts, words, and actions. All of life needs to be directed to him. To increase the student's understanding of "remember," the narrator used several descriptions of remembrance in verses 9–12.

"Remember" seems to have to do with a relationship with God rather than acquiring information about him. Two words in verses 9 and 10 are relational words—"wise" and "knowledge." "Besides being wise, the Teacher also taught the people knowledge, weighing, and studying and arranging many proverbs" (12:9). The narrator claimed that the teacher was wise. Wisdom in the Old Testament is not theoretical wisdom but practical wisdom. Godly wisdom does not come by intellectual study of God's character and ways. It comes as a gift of God through a relationship with him. It means insight that only comes from God. "The fear of the Lord is the beginning of wisdom, and the knowledge of the Holy One is insight" (Prov. 9:10). The Teacher was a wise man because of a relationship with God. Fortunately the Teacher did not keep his wisdom to himself. He shared it. He taught the people "knowledge." The knowledge the Teacher taught needs to be understood as more than the accumulation of facts. It is closely related to introducing people to the Creator. Ultimately, it is fellowship-knowledge that comes in the context of knowing someone.[3]

The narrator described Koheleth's techniques for teaching his students knowledge—weighing, studying, and arranging many proverbs. The word "weighing" indicates the careful evaluation of an idea. The word "studying" refers to the thoroughness and diligence of investigating something. Then after weighing and studying, the Teacher "arranged" ideas for the orderliness of his presentation. His medium was "many proverbs." The word "proverb" (*masal*) has a wide range of meaning. It could refer to a fable, a riddle, witticism, parable, crisp saying, parallelism, comparison, acrostic pattern, allegories, and rhetorical questions.[4]

The call to remembrance certainly has to do with relating the truth. "The Teacher sought to find pleasing words, and he wrote words of truth plainly" (12:10). The narrator related how the Teacher taught poetically. He wrote with "pleasing words." The word "pleasing" refers to something pleasant. The expression probably refers to artful expressions. Koheleth not only sought to find pleasing words, but he also wrote with "words of truth plainly." His work involved more than just aesthetically using "pleasing words." It involved a concern for the truth expressed by the pleasing words. The narrator does not say that Koheleth found the right words, but he sought to find them. He wrote the truth "plainly," which means honestly and graphically.

The call to remember the Creator involves an openness to correction. "The sayings of the wise are like goads, and like nails firmly fixed are the collected sayings that are given by one shepherd" (12:11). The goad was a large pointed stake used to prod an animal. Goads were used to direct the path of the animal and alter the animal's behavior when necessary. The words of the wise are like goads, there to spur an individual, to dig into one like "nails firmly fixed." Sometimes remembering the Creator

An Honest Look at Life: Ecclesiastes

involves hurtfulness. But the hurt is necessary for the person's good. People often need the correcting prick of a goad to strike home. It will lead them in the right direction, and it will correct them when they have gone the wrong way. Remembering the Creator involves allowing the Creator to have a real part in changing life. Attitudes, ambitions, relationships, and lifestyles need to come under the prodding of the goad. Without such correction life will remain meaningless.[5]

Remembering the Creator means a concentrated focus on his word. "Of anything beyond these, my child, beware. Of making many books there is no end, and much study is a weariness of the flesh" (12:12). Writing books was prevalent long before Ecclesiastes was written. Michael A. Eaton writes, "Writing was well established as a hallmark of civilization from about 3500 BC onwards."[6] Israel had much of the wisdom tradition of surrounding nations. They knew about pagan literature. The Teacher warns his students not to go beyond "the collected sayings." What does he mean by these collected sayings? One cannot be absolutely certain, but it could mean those writings recognized by the covenant community that have a unique inspiration and a practical application to life. "Of anything beyond these, my child, beware." Many good writings existed in Koheleth's day, but to remember God properly means to keep the divinely inspired writings preeminent. The intent in verse 12 is to inform readers that a lot which has been written is erroneous. Study of these books fail to enlighten, and they cause people to be weary.

Reason for Remembrance

12:13-14

The narrator turns from a critique of writings to what he believed the readers of Ecclesiastes should learn. He concludes what is of greatest importance to the readers. Ecclesiastes closes with motive clauses or reasons for remembering your Creator. Probably the reason for the final words is that the writer does not want anyone to be in doubt about the greatest significance of life. His statements are brief and to the point, and his words communicate the powerful reasons for remembering the Creator.

One should remember the Creator because this is what is of utmost importance in life. "The end of the matter; all has been heard. Fear God and keep his commandments; for that is the whole duty of everyone" (12:13). The sense of the verse is—end of discussion. The writer goes on to state the conclusion of the matter. What is writes is of primary importance. The ultimate commands in life are to "fear God" and "keep his commandments."

Koheleth had used the words "fear God" earlier in

Ecclesiastes (3:14; 5:7; 7:18; 8:12). Temper Longman III thinks that although Koheleth stated the words "fear God," it came from a rather doubtful position. Longman thinks that in this section the narrator asserted without doubt that the readers are to "fear God."[7] Fearing God does not mean to be terrified of God. It means to stand in awe of him. God is the Almighty Creator, and humans are mere creatures. God is absolutely holy, and humans are woefully sinful. God is eternal, and humans are a finite vapor. God is independent, and humans are dependent. Therefore, it is only fitting that human beings stand in awe of the eternal, almighty, Creator God.[8]

To fear God means to be in a relationship with him. It means to take him seriously, to honor and worship him. It means to place God in the center of one's existence.

Fearing God leads naturally to the next matter of utmost importance and that is keeping his commandments. A knowledge of God or a personal relationship with him leads to obedience. Proof of the relationship comes with the action of keeping his commandments. To acknowledge God as our Creator leads to doing what he says. Obedience results because of the relationship we have with a person. For example, sons obey their fathers because of the intimate relationship with the father.

The writer closes with two reasons for fearing God and keeping his commandments. The first reason is that it is "the whole duty of everyone." Actually the Hebrew literally reads "is the whole of everyone." It is not just our duty; it is the essence of our being. Augustine said, "You have made us for yourself and our heart is restless until it rests in you."[9] God made us in his likeness—human desire more and better than what the world gives. We cannot stuff the "God-shaped vacuum" with the things "under the sun" and expect to be satisfied. Fearing God and keeping his commandments are the most important things a person can do. There is no greater way to meaning and fulfillment and pleasure in life that fearing God and keeping his commandments. This is the way he made us.

The narrator gives a second reason for fearing and obeying God. It is because God will judge all of us. "For God will bring every deed into judgment, including every secret thing, whether good or evil" (12:14). Koheleth talked about judgment, but he never did develop the subject fully. The narrator asserts that God will make everything right with his judgment. At this point in the discussion, the narrator anticipates a judgment that will take place in the future. It will involve the evaluation of every secret thing, whether good or evil.

Koheleth spoke the last time in 12:1–7. His speech ended, and the anonymous narrator spoke up. His voice has not been heard since the prologue in 1:1–11. In the prologue the narrator simply set the mood and introduced

Koheleth's speech. In 12:8-14 the narrator concludes Ecclesiastes and evaluates what he has heard and who has spoken the words. Oddly enough the narrator has heard the speech of Koheleth. He commends him as a wise, professional person who worked hard and had good intentions. He affirms that Koheleth sought to find truth, though most of the truth Koheleth related was about life "under the sun." The narrator heard more from Koheleth than that life was vanity. He also heard positive truths about life. The narrator seems to summarize Koheleth's positive truths in three significant statements: fear God, obey his commands, and realize that God will judge.

The narrator introduced and concluded Ecclesiastes. He has exposed his child to the "under the sun" thinking of one wise man in Israel named Koheleth. The narrator did not discredit Koheleth's thinking. Koheleth did observe life under the effects of a rebellious humanity. He did see life as difficult, and then we die. The narrator would not let Ecclesiastes close on the subject of meaninglessness. He affirmed what Koheleth hinted thoughout Ecclesiastes, the need for a good relationship with God.

Bibliography

Barnes, Peter. *Both Sides Now: Ecclesiastes and the Human Condition*. Edinburgh: The Banner of Truth Trust, 2004.

Bartholomew, Craig G. *Ecclesiastes*. Baker Commentary on the Old Testament. Grand Rapids: Baker, 2009

Barton, George Aaron. *A Critical and Exegetical Commentary on the Book of Ecclesiastes*. The International Critical Commentary. Edinburgh: T. & T. Clarke, 1908.

Brown, William P. *Ecclesiastes*. Interpretation: A Bible Commentary for Teaching and Preaching. Louisville: John Knox, 2000.

Crenshaw, J. L. *Ecclesiastes*. Old Testament Library. Philadelphia: Westminster, 1987.

Davidson, Robert. *Ecclesiastes and the Song of Solomon*. The Daily Study Bible. Louisville: Westminster John Knox, 1986.

Eaton, Michael A. *Ecclesiastes*. Tyndale Old Testament Commentaries. Downers Grove, IL: InterVarsity, 1983.

Farmer, Kathleen A. *Who Knows What Is Good? A Commentary on the Books of Proverbs and Ecclesiastes*. Grand Rapids: Eerdmans, 1991.

Ferguson, Sinclair B. *The Pundit's Folly: Chronicles of an Empty Life*. Edinburgh: Banner of Truth Trust, 1995.

Fox, Michael V. *Ecclesiastes*. The JPS Commentary. Philadelphia: Jewish Publication Society, 2004.

_____. *A Time to Tear Down and a Time to Build Up: A Reading of Ecclesiastes*. Grand Rapids: Eerdmans, 1999.

Fredericks, Daniel C. and Daniel J. Estes. *Ecclesiastes & The Song of Songs*. Apollos Old Testament Commentary, vol. 16. Downers Grove, IL: InterVarsity, 2010.

Garrett, Duane A. *Proverbs, Ecclesiastes, Song of Songs*. The New American Commentary. Nashville: Broadman, 1993.

Greidanus, Sidney. *Preaching Christ from Ecclesiastes: Foundations for Expostiory Sermons*. Grand Rapids: Eerdmans, 2010.

Horne, Milton P. *Proverbs-Ecclesiastes*. Smyth & Helwys Bible Commentary. Macon, GA: Smyth & Helwys, 2003.

Hubbard, David Allen. *Beyond Futility: Messages of Hope from the Book of Ecclesiastes*. Grand Rapids: Eerdmans, 1976.

_____. *Ecclesiastes, Song of Solomon*. The Communicator's Commentary. Dallas: Word, 1991.

Jeremiah, David. *Searching for Heaven on Earth: How to Find What Really Matters in Life*. Nashville: Integrity Publishers, 2004.

Johnson, L. D. *Israel's Wisdom: Learn and Live*. Nashville: Broadman, 1975.

_____. *Proverbs, Ecclesiastes, Song of Solomon*. Layman's Bible Book Commentary. Nashville: Broadman, 1982.

Kaiser, W. C. *Ecclesiastes: Total Life*. Chicago: Moody, 1979.

Kidner, Derek. *The Message of Ecclesiastes*. The Bible Speaks Today. Downers Grove, IL: InterVarsity, 1985.

Knight, George R. *Exploring Ecclesiastes & Song of Solomon: A Devotional Commentary*. Hagerstown, MD: Review and Herald Publishing Association, 2006.

Kushner, Harold S. *When All You've Ever Wanted Isn't Enough*. New York: Summit Books, 1965.

Leupold, H. C. *Exposition of Ecclesiastes*. Grand Rapids: Baker, 1952.

Longman, Temper, III. *The Book of Ecclesiastes*. The New International Commentary on the Old Testament. Grand Rapids: Eerdmans, 1998.

_____. *Ecclesiastes/Song of Songs*. Cornerstone Biblical Commentary. Carol Stream, IL: Tyndale House Publishers, 2006.

Murphy, Roland E. *Ecclesiastes*. Word Biblical Commentary. Nashville: Thomas Nelson, 1992.

Peterson, Wayne H. *Ecclesiastes*. The Broadman Bible Commentary, vol. 5. Nashville: Broadman, 1971.

Provan, Iain. *Ecclesiastes/Song of Songs*. The NIV Application Commentary. Grand Rapids: Zondervan, 2001.

Rad, Gerhard von. *Old Testament Theology*. Vol. 1. Edinburgh: Oliver and Boyd, 1962.

Ryken, Philip Graham. *Ecclesiastes: Why Everything Matters*. Preaching the Word. Wheaton, Illinois: Crossway, 2010.

Seow, Choon-Leong. *Ecclesiastes*. Anchor Bible. New York: Doubleday, 1997.

Swindoll, Charles R. *Living on the Ragged Edge: Coming to Terms with Reality.* Waco, TX: Word, 1985.

Tidball, Derek. *That's Just the Way It Is: A Realistic View of Life from the Book of Ecclesiastes.* Ross-shire: England: Christian Focus, 1998.

Towner, W. Sibley. "Ecclesiastes." *The New Interpreter's Bible*, vol. 5, 265–360. Nashville: Abingdon, 1997.

Trible, Phyllis. "Ecclesiastes." *The Books of the Bible*, vol. 1, 231–39. Bernard W. Anderson, ed. New York: Charles Scribner's Sons, 1989.

Whybray, R. N. *Ecclesiastes.* The New Century Bible Commentary. Grand Rapids: Eerdmans, 1989.

Wiersbe, Warren W. *Be Satisfied: Looking for the Answer to the Meaning of Life.* Wheaton, IL: Victor Books, 1990.

Endnotes

Chapter 1

[1] Michael V. Fox, *Ecclesiastes: The Traditional Hebrew Text with the JPS Translation* (Philadelphia: Jewish Publication Society, 2004), ix.

[2] David Hubbard, *Ecclesiastes/Song of Solomon*, The Communicator's Commentary (Dallas: Word, 1991), 19–20.

[3] Fox, *Ecclesiastes*, xxxii.

[4] Temper Longman III, *The Book of Ecclesiastes* in The New International Commentary on the Old Testament (Grand Rapids: Eerdmans, 1998), 4–5.

[5] Ibid., 5.

[6] Cited in Derek Kidner, *A Time to Mourn and a Time to Dance: Ecclesiastes and the Way of the World* (Downers Grove, IL: InterVarsity, 1976), 14.

[7] David Hubbard, *Beyond Futility: Messages of Hope from the Book of Ecclesiastes* (Grand Rapids: Eerdmans, 1976), 8.

[8] Roger Norman Whybray, *Ecclesiastes*, The New Century Bible (Grand Rapids: Eerdmans, 1989), 4.

[9] Ibid., 9–10.

[10] William P. Brown, *Ecclesiastes*, Interpretation: A Bible Commentary for Teaching and Preaching (Louisville: John Knox, 2000), 8–9.

[11] Whybray, 13.

[12] Craig G. Bartholomew, *Reading Ecclesiastes: Old Testament*

Exegesis and Hermeneutical Theory (Rome: Pontifico Instituto Biblico, 1998), 263.

[13] George R. Knight, *Exploring Ecclesiastes and Song of Solomon: A Devotional Commentary* (Hagerstown, MD: Review and Herald Publishing Association, 2000), 19.

[14] Ibid., 12.

[15] Sidney Greidanus, *Preaching Christ from Ecclesiastes: Foundation for Expository Sermons* (Grand Rapids: Eerdmans, 2010), 12.

[16] Phyllis Trible, "Ecclesiastes," in *The Books of the Bible*, vol. 5, Bernard W. Anderson, ed. (New York: Charles Scribner's Sons, 1989), 232.

[17] William Sanford La Sor, David Allen Hubbard, and Frederic W. Bush. *Old Testament Survey: The Message, Form and Background of the Old Testament* (Grand Rapids: Eerdmans, 1982), 533–34.

[18] Longman, 20.

[19] Greidanus, 13–15.

[20] Fox, *Ecclesiastes*, 3.

[21] James L. Crenshaw, *Ecclesiastes*, Old Testament Library (Philadelphia: Westminster, 1987), 192.

Chapter 2

[1] W. Sibley Towner, "Ecclesiastes," *The New Interpreter's Bible*, vol. 5 (Nashville: Abingdon, 1997), 290–91.

[2] Ibid.

[3] Longman, 67.

[4] Ibid.

[5] Crenshaw, 64.

[6] Derek Tidball, *That's Just the Way It Is: A Realistic View of Life from the Book of Ecclesiastes* (Ross-shire, England: Christian Focus Publications, 1998), 16.

[7] Kidner, 25–26.

[8] Longman, 71.

[9] Ibid., 72.

[10] Gerhard Von Rad, *Old Testament Theology: The Theology of Israel's Traditions*, vol. 1, D. M. G. Stalker, trans. (San Francisco: Harper & Row, 1965), 455.

[11] Michael A. Eaton, *Eccclesiastes*, Tyndale Old Testament Commentaries (Downers Grove, IL: InterVarsity, 1983), 61.

Chapter 3

[1] Fox, *Ecclesiastes*, 7–8.

[2] Quoted in Fox, *Ecclesiastes*, 8.

[3] Longman, 83.

[4] Robert Davidson, *Ecclesiastes and the Song of Solomon*, The Daily Study Bible (Louisville: Westminster/John Knox, 1986), 14.

[5] Longman, 90.

[6] Wayne H. Peterson, *Ecclesiastes*, The Broadman Bible Commentary (Nashville: Broadman Press, 1971), 112.

[7] Longman, 106.

Chapter 4

[1] Eaton, 77.

[2] Quoted in Eaton, 78.

[3] Ibid.

[4] Longman, 114.

[5] Ibid., 115.

[6] Eaton, 79.

[7] Whybray, 71.

[8] Longman, 116.

[9] Brown, 42.

[10] Kidner, 39.

[11] Crenshaw, 100.

Chapter 5

[1] Greidanus, 98.

[2] Ibid, 99.

[3] Iain, Provan, *Ecclesiastes/Song of Songs*, The NIV Application Commentary (Grand Rapids: Zondervan, 2001), 103.

[4] Brown, 49.

[5] Charles R. Swindoll, *Living on the Ragged Edge: Coming to Terms with Reality* (Waco, Texas: Word Books, 1985), 112-29.

[6] Brown, 49.

[7] Richard J. Foster, *Freedom of Simplicity* (San Francisco: Harper & Row, 1981), 52-73,

[8] Longman, 142.

[9] Eaton, 94.

[10] Ibid, 95.

Chapter 6

[1] Milton P. Horne, *Proverbs/Ecclesiastes*, Smyth & Helwys Bible Commentary (Macon, GA: Smyth & Helwys, 2003), 449.

[2] Knight, 84.

[3] Alexander MacLaren, *Esther, Job, Proverb and Ecclesiastes*, Exposition of Holy Scripture (Grand Rapids: Eerdmans, 1998), 352.

[4] Brown, 55.

[5] Greidanus, 131.

[6] Quoted in Brown, 55.

[7] MacLaren, 353.

[8] Eaton, 100.

[9] Longman, 155.

Chapter 7

[1] Greidanus, 149.

[2] Saint Augustine, *Saint Augustine Confessions* (Oxford, England: Oxford University Press, n.d.).

[3] Kidner, 56.

[4] Ibid.

[5] Eaton, 103.

Chapter 8

[1] Peterson, 118.

[2] Longman, 170–71.

[3] Ibid., 171.

[4] Ibid., 172.

[5] Greidanus, 154.

[6] Michael Fox, *A Time to Tear Down and A Time to Build Up: A Reading of Ecclesiastes* (Grand Rapids: Eerdmans, 1999), 140.

[7] Longman, 173–74.

[8] Eaton, 108.

Chapter 9

[1] Kidner, 64.

[2] Ernest Becker, *The Denial of Death* (Florence, MA: Free Press, 1975), ix.

[3] Fox, Ecclesiastes, 44.

[4] Greidanus, 172.

[5] Eaton, 110.

[6] Tidball, 113.

[7] Longman, 187.

[8] Provan, 141.

[9] Ibid.

[10] Brown, 77.

[11] Kidner, 68.

[12] Provan, 152.

[13] Longman, 204.

[14] Fox, *Ecclesiastes*, 51.

[15] Greidanus, 196

[16] Eaton, 117.

Chapter 10

[1] M. Scott Peck, *The Road Less Traveled: A New Psychology of Love, Traditional Values and Spiritual Growth* (New York:

Touchstone, 1978), 15.

[2] Greidanus, 211.

[3] Kidner, 74.

[4] Whybray, 134.

[5] Longman, 219.

[6] Eaton, 123.

[7] Quoted in Longman, 223.

[8] Brown, 90–91.

Chapter 11

[1] Crenshaw, 159.

[2] Philip Graham Ryken, *Ecclesiastes: Why Everything Matters*, Preaching the Word (Wheaton, IL: Crossway, 2010), 206.

[3] Brown, 91.

[4] Fox, *A Time to Tear Down and a Time to Build Up*, 292.

[5] Whybray, 142.

[6] Ibid., 143.

[7] Greidanus, 236.

[8] Quoted in Harold S. Kushner, *When All You've Ever Wanted Isn't Enough* (New York: Summit Books, 1986), 82.

[9] Eaton, 129.

[10] Brown, 95.

[11] Eaton, 130.

[12] Brown, 96.

[13] Ibid., 97.

Chapter 12

[1] Sinclair B. Ferguson, *The Pundit's Folly: Chronicles of an Empty Life* (Edinburgh: Banner of Truth Trust, 1995), 3.

[2] Ryken, 232.

[3] Longman, 122.

[4] Nobert Lohfink, *Qoheleth*, Sean McEvenue, trans. Continental Commentaries (Minneapolis: Fortress, 2003), 125.

[5] Crenshaw, 175.

Chapter 13

[1] Longman, 256.

[2] Choon-Leong Seow, *Ecclesiastes*, The Anchor Bible (New York: Doubleday, 1997).

[3] Quoted in Brown, 101.

[4] Quoted in Brown, 102.

[5] Quoted in Davidson, 78–79.

[6] Greidanus, 271.

[7] Longman, 257.

[8] Davidson, 80.

[9] Ryken, 258–59.

[10] Ibid, 259.

[11] Eaton, 143.

[12] Davidson, 82.

[13] Ibid.

[14] Ibid.

Chapter 14

[1] Frederick Buechner, *A Room Called Remember* (San Francisco: Harper & Row, 1984), 2–3.

[2] Tidball, 194.

[3] Eaton, 153.

[4] Ibid.

[5] Tidball, 200–1.

[6] Eaton, 155.

[7] Longman, 282.

[8] Greidanus, 309.

[9] Augustine, *Confessions*.

www.ingramcontent.com/pod-product-compliance
Lightning Source LLC
Chambersburg PA
CBHW020353170426
43200CB00005B/154